**Murdock Learning Resource
Center
George Fox College**
Newberg, Oregon 97132

DEMCO

JOHN DEAR

Our god is Nonviolent

WITNESSES IN THE STRUGGLE FOR PEACE & JUSTICE

1990   The Pilgrim Press   New York

Copyright © 1990 by The Pilgrim Press
All rights reserved. No part of this publication may be reproduced, stored in a
retrieval system, or transmitted in any form or by any means, electronic,
mechanical, photocopying, recording, or otherwise (brief quotations used in
magazine or newspaper reviews excepted), without the prior permission of the
publisher.

Grateful acknowledgment is made by Pilgrim Press for use of the following:
Ched Myers, *Binding the Strong Man: A Political Reading of Mark's Story of Jesus.*
Used by permission of Orbis Books. James Douglass, *The Non-Violent Cross*
(New York: Macmillan & Co., 1968); *Resistance and Contemplation* (New York:
Doubleday & Co., 1972); *Lightning East to West* (New York: Crossroad, 1983).
Used by permission of James Douglass. William R. Watley, *Roots of Resistance:
The Nonviolent Ethic of Martin Luther King, Jr.* Used by permission of Judson
Press, Valley Forge, Pa. *A Testament of Hope: The Essential Writings of Martin
Luther King, Jr.*, edited by James M. Washington. Copyright © 1986 by
Coretta Scott King, Executrix of the Estate of Martin Luther King, Jr.
Reprinted by permission of Harper & Row Publishers, Inc. Walter Wink,
Violence and Nonviolence in South Africa: Jesus' Third Way. Copyright © 1987
New Society Publishers, Philadelphia, Pa., and Box 582, Santa Cruz, Calif.
95061. Used by permission. John Dear, "A Whisper in Our Hearts," from
Sojourners (Aug/Sept 1987). Portions of this work appeared originally as
"Gandhi's Experiments Today," in *The Catholic Worker* (Jan/Feb 1988), as "The
Experiments of Gandhi," in *Fellowship* (Jan/Feb 1988), as "Glorifying the God
of Peace: The Nonviolence of Thomas Merton," in *Fellowship* (Dec 1988), and
as "One Night in the Harlem Jail," in *The Catholic Radical* (Oct/Nov 1987).

Unless otherwise noted, Scripture selections are taken from the New American
Bible With Revised New Testament Copyright © 1986, by the Confraternity of
Christian Doctrine, Washington, D.C., and are used with permission.

Scripture quotations noted as such are from the Revised Standard Version of
the Bible, copyright, 1946, 1952, © 1971, 1973 by the Division of Christian
Education of the National Council of the Churches of Christ in the U.S.A.,
and are used by permission. For the purposes of inclusivity, these passages have
been amended.

Library of Congress Cataloging-in-Publication Data

Dear, John
    Our God is nonviolent : witnesses in the struggle for peace and justice /
John Dear.
        p.   cm.
    ISBN 0-8298-0852-3
    1. Nonviolence—Religious aspects—Christianity.   2. Peace—
Religious aspects—Christianity.   3. Christianity and justice.
I. Title.
BT736.6.D425   1990
241'.697—dc20
                                                        89-78142
                                                        CIP

The Pilgrim Press, 475 Riverside Drive, New York, N.Y. 10115

For Daniel Berrigan, S.J.
Brother,
I am glad
to keep Company
with you

Love your enemies and pray for those who persecute you, so that you may be sons [and daughters] of your Father [Mother] who is in heaven; for God makes the sun rise on evil and on the good, and sends rain on the just and unjust.

—Jesus (Matt. 5:44–45, RSV)

When the practice of nonviolence becomes universal, God will reign on earth as God does in heaven.

—Gandhi

Nuclear terror is there whether we like it or admit it. And if that is not unjust, wrong, evil—then nothing is. Further, if the Christian, who embodies the author and redeemer of life, doesn't address this issue with her or his life, then I fail to see how one professes Christ. Christ is God disarmed. We all, therefore, must disarm and be disarmed. . . . A Christian life is much more than written or spoken words. It is bearing the cross, a metaphor for nonviolent confrontation with a criminal superstate. Or two of them. As Christians, we dare not avoid the imperative of disarmament.

—Philip Berrigan

CONTENTS

Contents

ACKNOWLEDGMENTS

I would like to thank the 98th Street Jesuit Community in New York City and the K Street Jesuit Community in Washington, D.C. for the hospitality and support given to me as I wrote this book. I would also like to thank Janet and my brother, Stephen, for his assistance with this manuscript and for their inspiring work in Malawi, Africa; Jack, Kathy, Anne, Chris, Elmer, Edgar, and Peter, for all the fun along the way; my parents, David and Margaret Dear, for their constant support; George Anderson, S.J., Lisa Goode, Julie Turner, and everyone at St. Aloysius' Church in Washington, D.C. for their great spirit; Ed De-Berri, Ed O'Donnell, John Esseff, Adrian Barrett, and Maggie Ritz, for Scranton support; Dan and Cindy for Mt. Rainier; Shelley and Jim for friendship and example; Brother Patrick for the Gethsemani Retreat; Steve, Cindy, John, and Harry for Berkeley support; Mark Blackman and Mark Clarke for friendship and peacemaking; Brian and Pat for La Jolla, and Dave for all the support; Mary Lou and Dick for guidance and direction; Phil and Liz, for inspiration; Daniel, for making it possible, for all the encouragement and friendship; and Stephanie Egnotovich and Pilgrim Press for all the help.

Finally, I wish to extend my gratitude to all those communities of faith and resistance around the country who have shown me the hopeful possibility of creating a new world in the shell of the old: to everyone at Sojourners, the Catholic Worker communities, Jonah House, Pax Christi, the Fellowship of Reconciliation, the Open Door, CCNV, *Kairos*, the Plowshares movement, the Ground Zero and Metanoia communities—May God bless you all and grant you a strong, persevering faith and commitment to the gospel! Thank you for your lives.

FOREWORD

The indifference to crime committed against another is the infamy of the soul. Why does this happen—and among otherwise good and decent people? This question, however, begs another: Can we be good and decent people without passion, without caring about the people around us, without engaged concern for what happens in our world?

Our God is nonviolent, faithful to creation. And nonviolence is nothing if it is not fidelity to the living, if it does not encourage people to live and to tell the stories of their lives. This is why John Dear's book is so valuable. In it we read about "the scriptures of lives lived now, by the likes of us" (Dan Berrigan's insight). These stories create hope in a time when so many lives are unconsidered in our culture; when so many go down without a cry, their stories of no moment, because their lives are of no moment—dust filling the cracks. So I offer another story, one of seven lives. On Thanksgiving morning in 1983, seven normal people—not unlike you—enacted disarmament, rendering inoperable, for a time, a B-52 bomber, engines for that bomber, and engines for its escort planes. We focused on the B-52 because it is the delivery system for the Air Launched Cruise Missile (ALCM), an element of our nation's first-strike arsenal. We acted at Griffiss Air

Force Base because it was the first Strategic Air Command Base to outfit B-52s to carry these deadly Cruise Missiles. We, who came to be known as "The Griffiss Plowshares," were arrested, jailed, and later tried, convicted, and imprisoned for three years. Convicted we were—and are.

We disarmed the plane with hammers; we labeled it with blood. Was what we did violent? Violence wears a human face; it afflicts *people*. We hammered on a weapon of mass destruction, which we saw as anti-property, that is, as destroying, rather than "enhancing human life," which is how Mr. Webster defines property. This is not violence. How we treat the people named "oppressor" when we encounter them is the issue of violence and nonviolence. Nonviolence is persistent reconciliation. Biblically, reconciliation with all people is both the end and the means, but reconciliation is not possible with false gods, with idols, with the principalities and powers that rule the world. And the weapons carried in the B-52 are idols today or, as the Maryknoll film has it, "gods of metal."

We disarmed a weapon of mass destruction, but the real disarming went on among us, as we struggled to "give a reason for the hope that was in us" (1 Peter 3:15). We learned faith in one another; we breathed an atmosphere in which ideas, commitments, and symbols could be searched out; we were able to depend on people to do what they said; we waded through the skepticism that is a part of our culture. We became a community, witnessing thereby that human unity is indeed possible.

The spirit of disarmament was visible in the courtroom with friends, supporters, men and women of the press, and with the judge, the prosecutors, and the witnesses. Truth was spoken. Now, truth without love is violence; it hurts so much no one can hear it. It is abrasive. Conversely, love offered without truth is sentimentality, rotten to the core. Together, truth with love constitute the two-edged sword that can heal as it cuts deep into the person. Truth and love are geared to human community, to recreating and liberating. The structured antagonism of the courtroom was undermined by the spirit of community.

Our spirit of disarmament was tested in prison, where the brick and mortar walls and the chain link fences topped by barbed wire and concertina wire are the least one has to confront. We put our future in God's hands, arranged our lives so that something about a new humanity might flourish. Through all this, our community, vulnerable and clumsy as it was, was still evidence of the power of the Spirit. The Spirit of God working in us became a power in opposition to the power of the walls and of the weapons. We were free women and men, guests of a federally-funded peace camp! Such was our imprisonment.

We realized that there will be no disarmament—unilateral, bilateral, or multilateral—until there are people (and we have no idea how many will be required) who seek to be disarmed, until the spirit of disarmament grows among and within us. To be disarmed people, nonviolent people, we must be part of a process of recovering, restoring, and strengthening our spiritual tradition against the terrible pull of our culture with all its violence. Thus, the focus in Isaiah 2 and Micah 4.

Today, with tens of thousands of thermonuclear weapons ready for use about the globe, we must think of nonviolence as a process of disarmament, a process toward living disarmed lives. We come to understand that the weapons are not just "out there"—objects of unthinkable destruction—but that their source is in our own hearts and souls. They come out of our guts, out of the violence, the fear, the enmities between us, the walls we build against each other. As long as the walls stand, we will build weapons to defend them. In contrast, a disarmed life is a life without walls, without weapons, without enmity. It is an end. It is also a means, a conscientious process leading toward awareness of the walls we have built against one another, and our uprooting or transcending them.

Violence is nothing if not unimaginative. Nonviolence is as varied and imaginative as the lives that embrace it, as John Dear suggests. He introduces us to a handful of the people whose lives inform our search for truth and love. Read this book. Love these people. Look for more. Join the struggle!

ELIZABETH MCALISTER

Our God Is Nonviolent

INTRODUCTION

For an increasing number of Christians in the United States, the key to understanding Jesus' gospel in these nuclear times is through the practice of nonviolent resistance to war and injustice. Nonviolent resistance is a way of life and a way of liberation, a way taught and practiced by Jesus in the oppressed region of the Roman Empire where he lived. His message and activities led to his brutal murder, but, in faith, we Christians believe that he rose from the dead, and in that spirit of resurrection invited us to follow his way of nonviolent love and resistance unto our own deaths. For those who take up Jesus' way of life and who do so with the gift of their entire lives, such a change can bring many blessings, and persecutions as well.

In these days of the nuclear arms race, in an age where more than forty-five wars are being waged around the globe, in a time when 45,000 people starve to death every day, the necessity for the practice of nonviolence has taken on urgent proportions. Our world, in many ways, is addicted to violence and death; they have become the methods we use to relate to one another in time of conflict. The world spends $1.7 million every minute on weapons of death, over $800 billion annually. But like the addict, who kills himself, our addiction to violence and death now threatens to destroy the entire human race and the planet. Ever since August 6, 1945, when the United States dropped an atomic bomb on the people of Hiroshima, killing 130,000 people instantly, the world has been on the brink of another nuclear war. After the bomb was dropped on the people of Nagasaki on August 9, 1945, killing another 30,000 people, the United States government announced that such measures were necessary to save the lives of Americans. Historians have only recently uncovered a more truthful explanation: United States armed forces killed those people with those weapons not to force Japan to surrender but to prove to the Soviet government that the United States was militarily superior.[1]

In a sense, World War II never ended; it became the nuclear arms race. Today there are more than 55,000 nuclear weapons in the world, enough to destroy it fifteen times over. In our most fearsome nightmares we cannot imagine their power. The United States and the Soviet Union do not want the arms race to stop, for it allows them to control the poor of the world and to keep to themselves an unfair portion of the world's resources. Since 1945, the world has come to the brink of nuclear war twenty-seven times. As we head toward the twenty-first century, more and more nations are stockpiling nuclear weapons and threatening to use them. This addiction has left the world gravely ill. There is a way out, however, and a Healer who shows us the way.

Jesus lived a way of nonviolent love that challenged and overcame death with the power of life. His way of nonviolence and resistance is a way out of the darkness to which our violence has brought us. His way has been adopted by many and has been led by saintly and prophetic practitioners: Gandhi, Martin Luther King, Jr., Dorothy Day, Ita Ford, Maura Clarke, Dorothy Kazel, Jean Donovan, Thomas Merton, James Douglass, Daniel Berrigan, and many others. People are turning to the nonviolent Christ for practical direction on how to transform our world of violence into one of peace and justice. This involvement is crucial if we are ever to create a world without war and nuclear weapons.

This book is a meditation on the practice and teachers of nonviolence as it is rooted in Christ. My thesis is simple: our God is a God of love and is nonviolent; God calls us to be nonviolent toward one another in order to transform our world of violence and war. God's Spirit is

2

liberating people from their cultural addictions to greed, violence, and death, and enabling people of faith to turn to the Word of God and find the strength to say no to violence in all its forms and yes to peace, love, and truth. Through our faith and individual acts of peaceful resistance, God is working to redeem all people. This work of God is the revolution of the gospel, the transformation of society and humanity into a world of nonviolent love and truth. We begin this revolution with our refusal to kill, our refusal to be violent, our refusal to be unjust, in short, through nonviolent resistance and the love and truth that transform all violence. The goal is liberation itself—true freedom, life in the kingdom of God for all people, obedience to the will of God. Since freedom exists in love and truth given selflessly, a life of nonviolent resistance given over in love is a life of freedom, a gift from the God of nonviolence.

I hope my reflections here will serve as an introduction to those who are newly exploring ways to create a better, more just, more peaceful world. I offer them also as a simple, meditative study on the basic questions, What is nonviolent resistance? and Why do people spend their lives in that work? We can take stock of where we are now in the stuggle for justice and peace, and where we are going, by looking at the foundation on which we are standing and at those who have dedicated their lives to peace from that place. That foundation is our fundamental belief in the living God who is nonviolent and just, and who is revealed in the active life of Jesus. This book, then, is an effort to plumb the depths of the truth of the gospel by examining some prominent modern practitioners of that gospel and the invitation that flows to us from that truth. I hope readers will be led to a greater understanding and pursuit of this great, nonviolent God of ours who invites us to take up the task of nonviolence.

Chapters 1–3 reflect on the paradigms of nonviolent action and discuss nonviolent resistance in general. I examine the nonviolence of Jesus as the fullest revelation of God and God's nonviolence, and the witness of Gandhi, who is understood here not just as a practitioner, but as the reinventor of nonviolent resistance for modern times, a paradigm for our nuclear age.

Chapters 4–9 review and examine the writings and lives of prominent apostles and disciples of Christian nonviolence and resistance to evil: Martin Luther King, Jr.; Dorothy Day; Ita Ford, Maura Clarke, Dorothy Kazel, and Jean Donovan; Thomas Merton; James Douglass; and Daniel Berrigan.

Chapter 10 and the Conclusion offer my personal testimony and a concluding review of the meaning of this good news of nonviolence for our lives.

Notes

1. For the most complete study of the bombings of Hiroshima and Nagasaki and a U.S. intelligence report in the National Archives that contradicts the popular notion that the United States had to drop nuclear weapons on Japan, see Gar Alperovitz, *Atomic Diplomacy: Hiroshima and Potsdam* (New York: Simon & Schuster, 1965). For a short synopsis of his research, see "Did We Have to Drop the Bomb?" by Gar Alperovitz in the editorial section of *The New York Times*, August 3, 1989. For further reading, see Arthur J. Laffin and Anne Montgomery, *Swords into Plowshares* (San Francisco: Harper & Row, 1987); Robert Aldridge, *First Strike* (Boston: South End, 1983); idem, *Nuclear Empire* (Vancouver: New Star Books, 1989); Michio Kaku and Daniel Axelrod, *To Win a Nuclear War* (Boston: South End Press, 1987); and *Waging Peace*, ed. Jim Wallis (San Francisco: Harper & Row, 1982).

1

Nonviolent Resistance

A WAY OF LIFE,
A WAY OF LIBERATION

On September 9, 1980, Daniel Berrigan, Philip Berrigan, Carl Kabat, Dean Hammer, Elmer Maas, Anne Montgomery, Molly Rush, and John Schuchardt entered the General Electric Nuclear Missile Reentry plant in King of Prussia, Pennsylvania, where nose cones for the Mark 12A nuclear missile are made. They hammered on two nose cones, poured blood on documents, and offered prayers of peace. They were arrested shortly thereafter, underwent a jury trial, and were sentenced to prison terms of up to ten years. In a statement, the group, known as the Plowshares Eight, said they had gone to King of Prussia in order to "beat swords into plowshares, [and to] expose the criminality of nuclear weaponry and corporate piracy."

We commit civil disobedience at General Electric because this genocidal entity is the fifth leading producer of weaponry in the U.S. To maintain this position, G.E. drains $3 million a day from the public treasury, an enormous larceny against the poor. We wish also to challenge the lethal lie spun by G.E. through its motto, "We bring good things to life." As manufacturers of the Mark 12A reentry vehicle, G.E. actually prepares to bring good things to death. Through the Mark 12A, the threat of first-strike nuclear war grows more imminent. Thus G.E. advances the possible destruction of millions of innocent lives. . . . In confronting G.E., we choose to obey God's law of life, rather than a corporate summons to death. Our beating of swords into plowshares is a way to enflesh this biblical call. In our action, we draw on a deep-rooted faith in Christ, who changed the course of history through his willingness to suffer rather than to kill. We are filled with hope for our world and for our children as we join this act of resistance.[1]

Since that time, more than twenty-five other groups of concerned Christians and people of good will have "beat swords into plowshares" to resist the United States government's plans for nuclear war. At the trial of the Plowshares Eight, Daniel Berrigan asked himself, "Do you have anything to offer human life today?" His answer, he explained, was his action:

Our act is all I have to say. The only message I have to the world is: We are not allowed to kill innocent people. We are not allowed to be complicit in murder. We are not allowed to be silent while preparations for mass murder proceed in our name, with our money, secretly. I have nothing else to say in the world. At other times one could talk about family life and divorce and birth control and abortion and many other questions. But this Mark 12A is here. And it renders all other questions null and void. Nothing, nothing can be settled until this is settled. Or this will settle us, once and for all. It's terrible for me to live in a time where I have nothing to say to human beings except, "Stop killing." There are other beautiful things that I would love to be saying to people. There are other projects I could be very helpful at. And I can't do them. I cannot. Because everything is endangered. Everything is up for grabs. Ours is a kind of primitive situation, even though we would call ourselves sophisticated. Our plight is very primitive from a Christian point of view. We are back where we started. Thou shalt not kill; we are not allowed to kill. Everything today comes down to that— everything.[2]

"We are not allowed to kill." In a society that spends billions of dollars on war, weapons, and preparations for nuclear war, such a statement is revolutionary. For Daniel Berrigan and the Plowshares defendants, "everything comes down to this." Their act, their word, and their willingness to accept the consequences of their public statement point a way to liberation from the culture of violence and death, and a way to peace.

The way of life these peacemakers and millions of others have followed is the way of nonviolent resistance. Nonviolence is often misunderstood as passivity or quietism, but it is actually quite the opposite. Nonviolence is active love and truth; and in the face of violence, it resists. *Simply put, nonviolence is a way to fight against injustice and war without using violence. It is the force of love and truth that seeks change for human life, that resists injustice, that refuses cooperation with violence and systems of death. It is noncooperation with violence.* It says that the means are the ends, that the way to peace is peace itself. Nonviolent resistance is the willingness to take on suffering ourselves in order to right wrongs, in order to change the evil system of death that is all around us into freedom and life and love for everyone. The nonviolent resister makes a commitment never to kill, to be complicit in killing, to harm or threaten to harm anyone—no matter how great the cause, even if it appears to be for the kingdom of heaven. Further, she or he will seek to stop all forms of injustice.

Nonviolent resistance is liberating action on behalf of suffering humankind. It is an all-encompassing way of life whose tactics and methods may be applied to one's community, country, or the world. Nonviolent resistance is the act of nonretaliation while unmasking the violence of society. While this act requires a willingness to suffer, a willingness not to strike back, indeed, a willingness to die for truth, it seeks to free our adversary or adversaries—those brothers and sisters who support injustice or evil—by exposing all the violence and injustice that is hidden or covered up. As our adversaries begin to recognize our humanity, the sacrifices made, the risks taken, and the violence hidden in their practice of injustice or evil, their eyes may be opened and their own participation in the injustice becomes apparent to them. In that instant of recognition and subsequent shame, the violence and injustice can stop—forever.

Nonviolent resistance is an act of liberation from our enslavement to violence and injustice, into the freedom of life in the Spirit of God—the life of love and truth. This process of transformation, led by the

Spirit of God working through human beings, incorporates several characteristics.

Recognizing and Proclaiming the Injustice

Nonviolent liberating action for justice begins with consciousness-raising,[3] that is, informing others about our addiction to violence by speaking the truth publicly and questioning deception, injustice, or violence. In a society that aggressively hides its injustices and feeds on despair, consciousness-raising is an act of nonviolent resistance. One of the first tasks in beginning the lifework of nonviolent resistance in the U.S. is to study the reality of the evil we condone (such as the nuclear arms race, and our wars in Central America), to open our eyes and ears to the realities of the systemic violence and injustice and the realities of life for the poor and oppressed. We must question ourselves and then others. Injustices and violence must be publicly recognized and addressed through leafleting and dialogue in the public forum. Investigation, education, and negotiation are legal steps to take while seeking positive social change. It is only later, if this consciousness-raising has been attempted without success (as invariably, I believe, will happen), that the nonviolent resister may consider civil disobedience.

Jesus began his public ministry by announcing "good news of peace," that "the kingdom of God is at hand." His proclamation is a radically consciousness-raising invitation. This groundwork, based on love, truth, and trust in God, is the foundation of our future actions. A discerning spirit, that is, a posture of prayer that is open to God's movement within oneself and in one's peace community, is necessary in order to see how to best reveal the truth.

Danilo Dolci, the well-known nonviolent resister in Sicily, who confronted the unjust rule of the Mafia in his country, began first by asking questions. Gradually, he urged the people to think about their plight through a process that he called "popular self-analysis." His famous "strike in reverse" took place only much later. Unemployed Sicilian peasants, having recognized and analyzed the oppression they suffered, organized themselves and started to build roads on their own.

The government declared this "reverse strike" illegal, and all the "strikers" were placed in jeopardy. But through their nonviolent insistence on justice and their nonviolent opposition to the authorities, their work was eventually honored and the social change they sought became more of a reality.

Refusing to Cooperate with Evil

A second maxim of nonviolent resistance is the simple truth that noncooperation with evil is as much a duty as cooperation with good. The Montgomery, Alabama, bus boycott is an example of noncooperation with evil. The boycott of segregated buses in Montgomery began on December 1, 1955, when Rosa Parks refused to move to a back seat in a bus when a white male passenger demanded to have her seat in the front. Inspired by her act of resistance, blacks in Montgomery organized and publicly refused to cooperate with this manifestation of the evil of racism: segregated buses. As Martin Luther King, Jr., said later, noncooperation with this evil was simply a duty. What developed from this duty—the civil rights movement—continues today. At the time, however, no one dreamed that such a movement would either begin or succeed, as historian William Watley notes:

No one anticipated the gentle and soft-spoken Rosa Parks's action in refusing to yield her seat to a white male as she sat within the designated boundaries for black passengers on the local segregated bus. No one anticipated that it would be the arrest of Rosa Parks, the proverbial last straw in a long series of abuses borne by the black community, which would ignite the flame of revolt within it and mobilize it for concerted action. No one anticipated that a one-day boycott would stretch into a 382-day boycott which would end in a U.S. Supreme Court decision declaring segregation statutes of Montgomery buses to be unconstitutional. No one anticipated the national focus that would be turned on Montgomery blacks and their leadership as they sought to resolve a local problem. No one foresaw the significance of their actions and victory in challenging racism in all of its manifestations across America. No one anticipated the emergence of Martin Luther King, Jr., as a latter-day "Moses" or as the "American Gandhi" for this nation's liberal constituencies, politically, theologically, in both the black and the white communities.[4]

Serious nonviolent noncooperation with evil performed in conjunction with cooperation with good and in a spirit of love will bear good fruit in society. One of the first steps the nonviolent resister must take is to stop doing what is wrong, whether that be participation in the oppression of others, complicity in national or international oppression, or passive acceptance and tolerance of oppression. A person must consciously refuse to cooperate with anything that is evil. Noncooperation means resigning a military post or a job in the nuclear industry and then publicly beginning the process of noncooperation with every manifestation of that evil, whether that be by refusing to give up one's rightful seat on a segregated bus or by speaking out against nuclear war.

Noncooperation with evil includes the recognition that silence on the matter of the nuclear arms race, war, hunger, poverty, and the other ills of society is complicity with those evils. Though politicians and corporate authorities may claim to be against nuclear war, for instance, the continuing daily development of new nuclear weapons and more sophisticated first-strike strategies proves otherwise. The passive acceptance, silence, apathy, and indifference of millions of us in light of such growth in our nuclear capability and in the face of relievable human suffering is wrong. Noncooperation with complicity is the act of publicly saying no to the nuclear arms race and other current wars and injustices. Noncooperation with silence and apathy is a duty, as Gandhi said, when the masses are silent and when governments plan to destroy all life on earth. What is also implied in this Christian/Gandhian insight is that active noncooperation with evil will involve a struggle since one is attempting to break free from the tide of injustice and swim in another direction—to safety, to justice. Governments, which are never passive, will not stand idly by and permit noncooperation with state policies to continue: they will take action, usually criticism or harassment, and in some cases, arrest, imprisonment, or execution. The nonviolent resister knows however that in a time of evil and injustice, noncooperation with evil is not only a noble and just act, it is a duty and an obligation.

Loving One's Enemies

All liberating nonviolent action must be rooted in a deep respect for the opponent, and not in the need for the opponent's repudiation. This respect lies in the recognition of the divinity and humanity of every human being. Jesus called this aspect of liberating action "loving one's enemies," and placed it at the heart of his teaching. When the evangelists use the word "love," as in this case (Matt. 5:44–45), they deliberately use the Greek word *agape*, which means a willingness to lay down one's life in the nonviolent struggle for justice and peace for all, in the selfless service of all, and in unconditional, nonretaliatory love for the entire human family. The recognition of the ultimate worth of every human being, therefore, is a deep-seated appreciation of truth—the truth that all human beings are equal, that God is present in each of us, that every human being is redeemed by God. In this recognition is an acceptance of God's invitation to participate with God in God's work of redemption. Maintaining respect for the opponent, while nonetheless steadfastly clinging to truth and to justice, is essential to this redeeming love. In other words, in order to put into practice the belief that all humanity is one, that all are equal children of God, we must love those people who are the declared enemies of our country. When we stand with the victims of our own state, the risks will be great, but our common humanity will be affirmed and nonviolent love will be incarnated in a most dramatic form. Enemies are then transformed into friends.

It is precisely this "love of enemies"—this love for oppressors and opponents practiced while opposing injustice—that encourages nonviolent liberation theologians and activists to stand with the poor and the oppressed. Out of respect and love for both the oppressors and the oppressed, they side with the poor and seek, from this grounding, the liberation of the oppressed *and* the oppressors. They seek the liberation of the oppressed with whom they stand by loving them and by loving their enemies—the oppressors—to the point at which they will no longer oppress and then beyond that point to their conversion and transformation.

Latin American liberation theologian Gustavo Gutierrez explains this action on behalf of the victim and the victimizer:

To love all people does not mean avoiding confrontations; it does not mean preserving a fictitious harmony. Universal love is that which in solidarity with the oppressed seeks also to liberate the oppressors from their own power, from their ambition, and from their selfishness: "Love for those who live in a condition of objective sin demands that we struggle to liberate them from it. The liberation of the poor and the liberation of the rich are achieved simultaneously" (Girardi). One loves the oppressors by liberating them from their inhuman condition as oppressors, by liberating them from themselves. But this cannot be achieved except by resolutely opting for the oppressed, that is, by combatting the oppressive class. It must be a real and effective combat, not hate. This is the challenge, as new as the Gospel: to love our enemies. . . . It is not a question of having no enemies, but rather of not excluding them from our love. Love does not mean that the oppressors are no longer enemies, nor does it eliminate the radicalness of the combat against them. "Love of enemies" does not ease tensions; rather it challenges the whole system and becomes a subversive formula.[5]

True liberation occurs only when both oppressor and oppressed are set free. The nonviolent resister seeks liberation for the opponent, or enemy, so that they can live—together—in justice and peace, and even friendship.

This radical love of enemies and oppressors was clearly demonstrated in the life and works of Mohandas Gandhi, in particular in the relationship and friendship that he cultivated with his "enemies," such as Jan Christian Smuts, the leader of South Africa in the early 1900s. Toward the end of his life, Gandhi made the bold statement that he had long ago ceased to hate (even though many people oppressed and hurt him), and that he had always sought reformation, indeed redemption, for everyone:

I hold myself to be incapable of hating any being on earth. By a long course of prayerful discipline, I have ceased for over forty years to hate anybody. I know this is a big claim. Nevertheless, I make it in all humility. . . . But I can and do hate evil wherever it exists. I hate the system of government that the British people have set up in India. I hate the ruthless exploitation of India even as I hate from the bottom of my heart the hideous system of untouchability for which millions of Hindus have made themselves responsible. But I do not hate the domineering British as I refuse to hate the domineering Hindus. I seek to reform them in all the loving ways that are open to me. My noncooperation has its roots not in hatred, but in love.[6]

Gandhi's understanding of nonviolent resistance was rooted in the belief that the adversary is not an enemy to be overcome, but a participant in the search for a truthful solution to the conflict who needs to be "weaned from his error."[7] Indeed, Gandhi invented a new word to describe this commitment to truth. He began to speak of *satyagraha*, or truth-force.

[*Satyagraha* means] in essence the principle of nonviolent noncooperation. It . . . must have its root in love. Its object should not be to punish the opponent or to inflict injury upon him. Even while noncooperating with him, we must make him feel that in us he has a friend and we should try to reach his heart by rendering him humanitarian service wherever possible. . . . Although noncooperation is one of the main weapons in the armory of satyagraha, it should not be forgotten that it is, after all, only a means to secure the cooperation of the opponent consistently with truth and justice. . . . Avoidance of all relationship with the opposing power, therefore, can never be a satyagrahi's object, but transformation or purification of that relationship.[8]

The way in which Gandhi developed a friendly relationship with Smuts, the South African leader, is a classic example of Gandhi's noncooperation rooted in love. In 1914, when Gandhi left South Africa after many years of struggling for justice and disturbing the "peace" of South Africa, he left a gift for General Smuts: a pair of sandals that Gandhi had made while in prison. Smuts wore them every summer for years afterward. In 1939, on Gandhi's seventieth birthday, Smuts returned the sandals to him "as a gesture of friendship." Smuts said of Gandhi, "He never forgot the human background of the situation, never lost his temper or succumbed to hatred, and preserved his gentle humor even in the most trying situations. His manner and spirit even then, as well as later, contrasted markedly with the ruthless and brutal forcefulness which is the vogue in our day." Referring to Gandhi's gift, Smuts declared, "I have worn these sandals many a summer since then, even though I may feel that I am not worthy to stand in the shoes of so great a person."⁹

Reflecting on the beauty of resistance rooted in nonviolent love, Gandhi wrote:

It is the acid test of nonviolence that in a nonviolent conflict there is no rancor left behind and, in the end, the enemies are converted into friends. That was my experience in South Africa with General Smuts. He started with being my bitterest opponent and critic. Today, he is my warmest friend . . . ¹⁰

Martin Luther King, Jr., was equally committed to the truth that oppressors must be liberated from their oppressing actions through the nonviolent resistance of the oppressed. King discovered that, by loving and respecting the opponent, the nonviolent resisters first find in themselves a new sense of strength and dignity, the first step in an almost natural progression.

The nonviolent approach does not immediately change the heart of the oppressor. It first does something to the hearts and souls of those committed to it. It gives them new self-respect; it calls up resources of strength and courage that they did not know they had. Finally, it reaches the opponent and so stirs his conscience that reconciliation becomes a reality.¹¹

Loving one's enemies can also mean moving beyond one's national borders into any foreign region marginalized and brutalized by one's country. For United States citizens, it can take the form of visiting and befriending people in the Soviet Union, and joining them in the work of disarmament; or living with the peasants of Nicaragua who have lived under the threat of U.S.-backed contra attacks. Such active love for the enemies of one's country enfleshes nonviolence and literally make peace in our world.

Ultimately, this "love of enemies" commended by Jesus, Gandhi, King, and others is the heart of life, reconciliation, and nonviolence. It is a radical love that respects all other human beings even while it seeks to transform a situation of violence and oppression into justice. The only way to a loving, reconciled community of peoples is through this nonviolent love. The means are the ends: enemies need to be loved now in order to be loved in the future as friends.

Voluntary Suffering as a Force of Redemption

True reconciliation can never be accomplished by inflicting pain and suffering on others, but only through nonviolent love. The *agape* love of the nonviolent struggle for truth, justice, and peace is characterized by the willing acceptance of personal suffering rather than violent retaliation and killing. This voluntary suffering in love is best demonstrated by Jesus Christ on the cross as he resisted the forces of death and darkness with total, bottomless love. Christ has been winning over hearts throughout the centuries because of his selfless love for all humanity demonstrated in his acceptance of violence and his nonviolent response to it.

The deepest understanding of this truth about nonviolent liberation is reached by experiencing and practicing suffering love in action. Many saints and martyrs, from Stephen and Peter to Jean Donovan, Dorothy Day, Oscar Romero, and Gandhi, have recognized in this truth a way to live love in action. Martin Luther King, Jr., demonstrated redemptive suffering love in his willingness to suffer the pain inflicted by opponents and in his response of love, forgiveness, and truth rather than further violence. For years, King struggled against the evils of racism and hatred, and suffered the pains of persecution for his commitment to the truth. His home was bombed; his family was threatened. His life was in danger almost daily. He was mocked, struck at, and stabbed, yet he refused to retaliate. Finally he was assassinated. He explained his nonviolent response this way:

Every time I see [hate], I say to myself, hate is too great a burden to bear. Somehow we must be able to stand up before our most bitter opponents and say: "We shall match your capacity to inflict suffering by our capacity to endure suffering. We will met your physical force

15

with soul force. Do to us what you will and we will still love. We cannot in all good conscience obey your unjust laws and abide by the unjust system, because noncooperation with evil is as much a moral obligation as is cooperation with good; and so, throw us in jail and we will still love you. Bomb our homes and threaten our children, and, as difficult as it is, we will still love you. . . . Be assured that we'll wear you down by our capacity to suffer, and one day we will win our freedom. We will not only win freedom for ourselves, we will so appeal to your heart and conscience that we will win you in the process, and our victory will be a double victory![12]

This willingness to accept suffering while clinging to the truth lay at the heart of King's teachings. Throughout King's liberation campaigns in the South, he would quote Gandhi: "Rivers of blood may have to flow before we gain our freedom, but it must be our blood." "Unearned suffering is redemptive" became his overriding theme at every prayer service the night before a march or an act of nonviolent civil disobedience. "Along the way of life, someone must have sense enough and morality enough to cut off the chain of hate. This can only be done by projecting the ethic of love to the center of our lives," King proclaimed.[13]

Reflecting on Gandhi's and Christ's steadfast acceptance of unearned suffering as the way to true liberation, theologian and peace activist James Douglass explained this "logic of nonviolence" as "the logic of crucifixion" in his book *The Nonviolent Cross:*

The purpose of nonviolence is to move the oppressors to perceive as human beings those whom they are oppressing. People commit acts of violence and injustice against others only to the extent that they do not regard them as fully human. Nonviolent resistance seeks to persuade the aggressor to recognize in his victim the humanity they have in common, which when recognized fully makes violence impossible. This goal of human recognition is sought through the power of voluntary suffering, by which the victim becomes no longer a victim but instead an active opponent in loving resistance to the person who has refused to recognize him or her as a person. The person of nonviolence acts through suffering love to move the unjust opponent to a perception of their common humanity, and thus to the cessation of violence in the commencement of brotherhood and sisterhood. The greater the repression, the greater must be the suffering courted by its victims; the greater the inhumanity, the greater the power of suffering love necessary to begin restoring the bonds of community. Suffering as such is powerless. Love transforms it into the kind of resistance capable of moving an opponent to the act of mutual recognition we have described. The suffering of his victim must be acknowledged by the oppressor as being human before he will cease inflicting it, and it is the love manifested in that suffering undergone openly and voluntarily which will bring him finally to this acknowledgment.[14]

Perhaps one of the clearest demonstrations of unearned suffering accepted by the victims in order to bring about justice and reconciliation was the nonviolent raid on the Dharasana Salt Works in India by the followers of Mohandas Gandhi on May 21, 1930. Row after row of trained nonviolent resisters walked forward to the entrance of the British-run salt mines only to be beaten severely by British soldiers and Indian guards hired by the British police. After each resister was beaten down or killed and then carried away by volunteers, a new group walked forward. United Press correspondent Webb Miller recorded that he "could detect no signs of wavering or fear" in the marchers: they "simply walked forward until struck down."[15] The brutality accepted yet resisted by the marchers touched the world and this incident proved to be one of the turning points on the road to the liberation of India from British domination.

Connected with this willingness to accept suffering for justice' sake is the willingness to live standing with and serving those who suffer and are oppressed, thereby expressing solidarity with the oppressed throughout the world. This life of solidarity with the poor and oppressed provides the setting for a life of nonviolent resistance to the injustice of society and inspires a willingness to suffer for love of the needy, as Dorothy Day demonstrated. It is an effort to identify with the least, the most marginalized, in all humanity, as Jesus did by identifying with the poor, the hungry, the homeless, the naked, the imprisoned, and the sick. This solidarity with the poor as a life act of loving resistance and nonviolence will entail varying degrees of suffering the oppression the poor suffer, but will speed up the day of liberation and justice.

Divine Obedience: Exposing
Latent Violence

Direct nonviolent action for justice and peace is provocative: it seeks "creative tension" in order to uncover latent violence and transform it into justice and love. Nonviolence reveals false peace for what it is: a cover-up for underlying hostilities, injustices, prejudices, and wars. Just as the march on the Dharasana Salt Works was provocative, so too was Gandhi's simple yet profound two-hundred-mile walk to the sea where he and his friends, in public defiance of British rule, gathered salt from the sea in order to claim their rights and not give in to oppression. The march created a wave of tension throughout India, provoking the British to respond. The sustained civil disobedience and resistance that followed forced the British to react. The British could have responded with even greater oppression, but instead were empowered over a period of several years, through the campaign of nonviolent revolution, to put down their instruments of violence and depart as friends.

Provocative nonviolent action for peace with justice often takes the public, communal form of civil disobedience, disobeying unjust laws in order to return a community to a higher just law. It is undertaken with complete knowledge and acceptance of the consequences. Christian communities have begun to term this obedience to God's law of love "Divine Obedience." Dorothy Day's divine obedience led to repeated imprisonment. Her public refusal in the 1950s to participate in the preparation for nuclear war by going underground into New York air raid shelters forced people to confront the reality that they were choosing to ignore: no one is safe from nuclear war. Day and her colleagues sat outside on park benches above ground during those air raid drills and were repeatedly arrested and jailed for their provocative action. The drills were eventually stopped because of these demonstrations and the awareness they raised.

Martin Luther King, Jr.'s divine obedience took the form of provoking white society in the United States to confront its system of racism. The public march, which included young children, during the campaign for civil rights in Birmingham provoked the entire nation to recognize and acknowledge some of its racist attitudes and behavior.

During the campaign, television news viewers watched as young marchers and activists were hosed down, attacked by dogs, and beaten. The violence that King and his nonviolent followers uncovered shocked the nation. They continued until their specific demands for justice were met.

King once related a conversation from the campaign in Montgomery, Alabama, which explained his mission to liberate society from latent violence through nonviolent direct action. A white man in Montgomery had challenged King, saying, "For all these years, we have been such a peaceful community; we have had so much harmony in race relations and then you people have started this movement and boycott and it has done so much to disturb race relations. We just don't love the Negro like we used to love them, because you have destroyed the harmony and the peace that we once had in race relations." King responded:

Sir, you have never had real peace in Montgomery. You have had a sort of negative peace in which the Negro too often accepted his state of subordination. But this is not true peace. True peace is not merely the absence of tension; it is the presence of justice. The tension we see in Montgomery today is the necessary tension that comes when the oppressed rise up and start to move forward toward a permanent, positive peace.[16]

It was in the North, however, that King discovered a deeper spirit of violence. Following his mission to uncover latent violence, King moved into a Chicago ghetto and began to take his nonviolent campaign for liberation to white suburbia. It was there that King saw, as he claimed, one of the strongest expressions of violence that he had ever encountered in his life. On August 5, 1966, King led six hundred blacks and whites into the all-white Marquette Park section outside of Chicago, where they were met with shouts, rocks, bottles, and bricks. With every green lawn and white house the marchers passed, the violence got worse. A few minutes later, a knife was thrown at King, just missing him and striking a white onlooker instead. When critics charged him with provoking violence, King responded as he had throughout the South: "We do not seek to precipitate violence. However, we are aware that the existence of injustice in society is the existence of violence, latent violence. We feel we must constantly expose this evil, even if it brings violence upon us." If violence is brought out into the open, King maintained, "then the community will be forced to deal with it."[17]

Direct nonviolent action may appear only to provoke, or even alienate, opponents and observers. But if it is truly rooted in nonviolent love, it will lead to a revelation: the truth about society and its violence and oppression, and the silence that often accompanies them. And then the necessary reconciliation will follow. First hearts and minds will be changed, then the policies and systems that perpetuate the injustice will be altered.

In their willingness to provoke society to move away from its violent tendencies, whether latent or manifest, nonviolent liberationists such as Day, Gandhi, and King displayed a courageous spirit of fearlessness. They were able to look society and its defenders in the eye and point out their underlying hostility and violent intentions. Despite intimidation, threats, and persecution directed at their campaigns, and indeed against their lives and the lives of their co-workers, they refused to respond with society's typical violence. They stood up without fear and unmasked society's intent to murder. Such fearlessness and boundless courage are necessary prerequisites for the nonviolent resister. When such nonviolent actions are combined with a radical openness to the truth and to dialogue, and with a deep respect for all people, the only possible outcome can be true liberation and justice.

The Disciplines of Nonviolent Resistance

Intimately connected with the way of life that is nonviolent resistance—a continuing openness to liberation—is the practice of spiritual discipline, daily prayer and contemplation. The saints and monks of the world's great religions have long held that true liberation will ultimately come from a life of prayer and the disciplines that go hand in hand with prayer—solitude and fasting. Such disciplines will open a way to inner unity and integrity, allowing the nonviolent resister to become an even greater channel of God's grace for the world.

In the life of a modern messenger of nonviolence, the monk Thomas Merton, we find this insistence on prayer and contemplation in everything he had to say concerning the struggle for justice and liberation. Merton's simple daily discipline of prayer and solitude was an experiment in nonviolence. Through his pursuit of the contemplative life as resistance to violence, he discovered a spirit of peace and a sense of freedom that he then wanted to share with the world. His discovery was for him a way to God. In his hermitage, he learned that the nonviolent life begins with prayer, solitude, and fasting.

Gandhi knew this, too, and frequently said that his greatest weapon in the nonviolent struggle for justice and peace was mute prayer. The courage and fearlessness required to accept suffering without retaliation in pursuit of justice can only be enacted by a lively faith in God and in God's reign of justice and love. Only with this belief and the constant recourse to God and God's mercy will the life of the nonviolent resister bear fruit. To achieve this, Gandhi scheduled daily prayer services into his busy life, and at least once a week kept silence for twenty-four hours.

Prayer is the first step in living out the presence of God and following the path of nonviolence. "Prayer from the heart can achieve what nothing else can in the world," Gandhi said on one occasion.[18] Gandhi's prayer came from a serious immersion in the *Bhagavad Gita* and the Sermon on the Mount. In the *Bhagavad Gita,* he found the key to the world of nonviolence: renounce everything for the love of serving others. Gandhi's practice of daily meditation on the second chapter of the *Bhagavad Gita* facilitated both his inner transformation and his ability to live a life of steadfast nonviolence. They enabled him to pursue his lifelong goal: "To see God face to face."

All of Gandhi's political actions came from following this path of life: renunciation of selfish desire, service to others, meditation on love and truth—God. In this way, prayer became for Gandhi a way of life. His life—in all its public features—involved a constant awareness of the reality of the spiritual dimension of life.

Gandhi and Merton both learned that nonviolent action springing from a life of discipline and prayer will flourish naturally as a result of a person's inner unity. Merton wrote, "The whole Gandhian concept of nonviolent action and satyagraha is incomprehensible if it is thought to be a means of achieving unity rather than as the fruit of inner unity already achieved."[19] Merton noted that Gandhi recognized this failure in his own campaign at the end of his life:

Gandhi saw that his followers had not reached the inner unity that he had realized in himself, and that their satyagraha was to a great extent a pretense, since they believed it to be a means to achieve unity and freedom, while he saw that it must necessarily be the fruit of inner freedom. The first thing of all and the most important of all was the inner unity, the overcoming and healing of inner division, the consequent spiritual and personal freedom, of which national autonomy and liberty would only be consequences. However, when satyagraha was seen only as a useful technique for attaining a pragmatic end, political independence, it remained almost meaningless. As soon as the short-term end was achieved, satyagraha was discarded. No inner peace was achieved, no inner unity, only the same divisions, the conflicts and the scandals that were ripping the rest of the world to pieces.[20]

A Matter of the Heart

Through their lifelong experiments in truth, Gandhi, Merton, and Dorothy Day discovered what Jesus preached and lived to the fullest: at the heart of nonviolent resistance is a nonviolent heart.

To begin to resist the injustice of the arms race and the evils of our political system, people must begin in their hearts, by resisting those forces within each of us that create violence. Nonviolence of the heart must be cultivated. People must be "reduced to zero," emptied of all violence, ego, and selfish desire.

Nonviolence of the heart refers to this state of zero, when a person has let go of ego and control and has nothing left. With this emptiness comes compassion, and this compassion is the first fruit of a nonviolent heart. Compassion in today's world of violence *is* nonviolent resistance in its deepest sense. Compassion as the fruit of emptiness and prayer means human liberation. Thus, from a simple, pure heart, rooted and grounded in love, a person can seek truly to build peace.

From here, one can move toward a world without weapons and war, a world free from fear, injustice, and the threat of nuclear annihilation.

Become reduced to the level of zero and accept the gift of a nonviolent heart in order to attempt any act of public resistance, Gandhi advocated. One cannot seek nonviolent love in the world without seeking it and allowing it to take root and grow in one's own heart. This is at the heart of the struggle. This is life in its fullest dimension: a change of heart. For when one accepts love and nonviolence in one's empty heart, then the doors of life are opened. Everyone is a sister or a brother, an image of God, a child of God. The poor are embraced and welcomed with special warmth and given everything. The truth can be told; forgiveness can be given and accepted; disarmament can begin. Suffering can be accepted willingly and transformed into a gift of love that will bear fruit in humanity. Arrest and imprisonment for nonviolent resistance become doors to freedom. Death becomes the door to resurrection. There is no such thing as defeat. Nonviolent resistance, then, is based in hope, in a vision like the dream of Martin Luther King, Jr., of a new life, a new age, a new world, in which all will be treated as one, as brothers and sisters, everyone as a child of God.

Such humility, a heart reduced to zero, the heart of nonviolent resistance, will have social and political consequences, as Jesus discovered and realized on Calvary. It will be understood by the warmaking state as dangerous. When the state then seeks to silence and crush the nonviolent heart, love and truth continue to rise and bloom. In other words, peace, love, and truth begin in the heart and flow out from this center into the world—not the other way around. This depth of nonviolence and resistance in the heart of the individual become over time a way of life, a path that is constantly, consistently chosen as the right and necessary road. Faithfulness to this narrow path of love and truth in the heart, rooted in faith and hope, will touch many other hearts and transform the world. In such faith and hope, the nonviolent resister can dream and envision formerly unforeseen possibilities. The goal of reconciliation will be lived out in one's own life. The common ground of humanity covered over by enmity, racism, sexism, classism, and injustice will be uncovered and revealed for what it is, a gift from God. We will learn that we are all one, already reconciled. The goal of nonviolence then is never victory for the resister, but reconciliation, redemption, justice for all concerned, liberation, and the transformation of society into the beloved community that we have been created to be. The way of liberation happens when human beings see one another and love one another as human beings. The liberation of the human being happens when the person clings to her or his identity as a human being—a child of God. Claiming one's identity, fundamentally, involves recognizing that one is powerless before the world and, then, holding onto that powerlessness as one's very life. Nonviolent liberation is this powerlessness accepted with love on behalf of suffering humanity, truth, and justice.

Nonviolent liberation is a gift from God who is nonviolent and a liberator. The God of nonviolence and liberation and life resists evil, practices nonviolent noncooperation with injustice, and stands in solidarity with the victims of injustice. In the lives of Jesus and Gandhi, the way to this God was revealed—through the cross, through satyagraha, through voluntary acceptance of suffering and powerlessness as the means to overcome evil with good. It is this life—life on the cross, in satyagraha—to which the nonviolent resister is ultimately wedded and this life is most fully lived and revealed in the life of Jesus.

Martin Luther King, Jr., eloquently summed up the human situation for our generation: "The choice is no longer between violence or nonviolence. Today, the choice is between nonviolence or nonexistence." If we are to live decent human lives, and if we are to be freed from our addiction to war and nuclear violence, we must move toward nonviolence as a way of life. We must resist our use of violence and our unjust practices and systems. As we take the road of nonviolence, we must delve deeper into the Spirit of nonviolence, the Spirit of God. We Christians need to study the scriptures and the lives of those Christians who have gone before us as messengers of truth and justice. We need to pray and to act on that prayer for peace.

Christians in the nuclear age need to take a new look at the life of Jesus and at common understandings of Christian discipleship. Seen through the eyes of nonviolent resistance to evil, the life of Jesus is a call to active nonviolence here and now. Jesus' life is a revelation of God as a God of nonviolent love, a God of resistance, a God of justice and peace. Let us turn, then, to the witness of Jesus to see that revelation.

Notes

1. Daniel Berrigan, *Portraits* (New York: Crossroad, 1984), 147, 158.
2. Jim Wallis, *Peacemakers* (San Francisco: Harper & Row, 1983), 154.
3. Belden C. Lane, "Spirituality and Political Commitment: Notes on a Liberation Theology of Nonviolence," *America* (March 14, 1981): 197–202.
4. William Watley, *Roots of Resistance* (Valley Forge, Pa.: Judson Press, 1985), 53–54.
5. Gustavo Gutierrez, *A Theology of Liberation* (Maryknoll, N.Y.: Orbis Books, 1973), 275–76.
6. Eknath Easwaran, *Gandhi the Man* (Petaluma, Calif.: Nilgiri Press, 1978), 56.
7. Ibid., 158.
8. Ibid.
9. Louis Fisher, *The Life of Mahatma Gandhi* (San Francisco: Harper & Row, 1950), 117–18.
10. Easwaran, *Gandhi the Man*, 163.
11. Coretta Scott King, ed., *The Words of Martin Luther King, Jr.* (New York: Newmarket Press, 1983), 79.
12. Ibid., 72.
13. Stephen Oates, *Let the Trumpet Sound: The Life of Martin Luther King, Jr.* (New York: New American Library, 1982), 79.
14. James Douglass, *The Nonviolent Cross* (New York: Macmillan Co., 1966), 71.
15. Ibid., 66–69.
16. Oates, *Let the Trumpet Sound*, 84.
17. Ibid., 411.
18. Thomas Merton, *Gandhi on Nonviolence* (New York: New Directions, 1964), 28.
19. Ibid., 6.
20. Ibid.

2

A Testament of Nonviolence

THE WITNESS OF JESUS

Each day, more and more searching Christians and people of good will are beginning to reexamine the scriptures for clues to the meaning of life and for ways to overcome the deadly addictions that continue to plague our culture. Poverty, societal violence, the horrors of war, and the nuclear arms race are forcing people to return to basic spiritual questions, such as, Who is God, anyway? Who is this Jesus of the Gospels? What does it really mean to follow Jesus today in a world of megadeath and rampant poverty? What are the serious political implications of our Christianity in light of this new age?

In the United States, the renewed search for God and a deeper understanding of Jesus' life are bearing fruit in a new witness of active nonviolence. Christians are rediscovering the ancient truth that God is a God of active nonviolent love, a God of the poor, a God who resists evil by making peace. Christians are discovering a "new" Jesus, and the truth that Jesus' life and teachings of two thousand years ago make sense for us today. It is crucial to review this new understanding of God and Jesus, gained from ancient scriptures, to understand the new movements of justice and peace in the United States.

For Christians, the witness of Jesus is our clue to the work of nonviolence we are called to enact. What we are learning is something that has the power to transform our very lives and the world as well. The Jesus of the Bible worshiped and obeyed a God who is compassionate, and knew God intimately through acts of justice and peace. The Jesus of the Gospels, who is the image of God in human history, we are discovering anew, is not a heavenly, pious figure, out of touch with the world's problems. Rather, he is a poor person in an oppressed region, passionately concerned with the suffering people of the world and with justice. He practiced steadfast, loving nonviolent resistance and civil disobedience; he was arrested, tried, and condemned to death because of such loving disobedience to authority; he was obedient to God's law of nonviolent love; and he overcame the powers of death through the resurrecting power of God's nonviolent love.

Let me say from the outset that of all the various schools of biblical study, I find myself most completely in agreement with the "new school" that is emerging among those Christians who are struggling here in the United States to resist nonviolently the powers of violence. That new theology has been called "sociopolitical hermeneutics," "liberation reading of the scripture," or, in the words of Ched Myers, "a socio-literary reading strategy for scripture," which sees the gospel narrative as a whole, and approaches it within the political context of its day and our day.

Perhaps the best book to date on this critical reading of scripture is Myers's *Binding the Strong Man: A Political Reading of Mark's Story of Jesus*. This book has reset the stage for biblical study and approach. Drawing upon the foundations of such scholars as John Howard Yoder, Norman Gottwald, Andre Trocme, G.H.C. MacGregor, William Stringfellow, Adela Collins, John Collins, Jon Sobrino, Walter Wink, and Fernando Belo, among others, Myers thoroughly analyzes the Gospel of Mark, the earliest of the Gospels, discovering it to be "a manifesto for radical discipleship," "an ideological narrative," and "the manifesto of an early Christian discipleship community in its war of myths with the dominant social order and its political adversaries."[1]

Myers uses the lens of "revolutionary nonviolence" to read Mark's story of Jesus and concludes that it is indeed a political manifesto for a nonviolent movement of resistance to tyranny. Written for a community committed to "nonaligned radicalism" at odds with every variety of oppression, Mark's Gospel, according to Myers, was meant to encourage those disciples to take up the cross of active nonviolent resistance to the powers of death on earth. Myers's book deserves serious study by scholars and peace activists, theologians as well as "average" American churchgoers. It was written by a nonviolent resister, in the praxis of nonviolent resistance to evil, for Christian communities of nonviolent resistance to evil, and, in the process, uncovered a treasure of revelation about Jesus from which the worldwide Christian community can benefit. Indeed, Myers has brought the Gospel alive again. Myers's book has become a rigorous, scholarly manifesto for radical discipleship in our own day, a discipleship that takes seriously the cross of nonviolent resistance to evil. It should pave the way for similar new political readings of other scripture texts.

Myers and other scholars are uncovering a much more radical, demanding Jesus than most people have been willing to accept.[2] The Gospels, we learn, portray a nonviolent revolutionary who is not aligned with any special group, who opposes every manifestation of institutionalized injustice, who worships a nonviolent God who loves *everyone*, especially the victim, the oppressed, the marginalized poor. This Jesus, we are told, says, "Follow me." Such an invitation is as radical, demanding, and possible today as it was in Jesus' time.

Jesus knew the Hebrew scriptures well and announced that he had come to fulfill the law of those scriptures and the truth proclaimed by its prophets of peace. His message revealed an image of God as a God of love and truth, a God who suffers for justice' sake, a God who defends the poor and the oppressed. From these roots, Jesus proclaimed good news of nonviolent resistance. He was murdered for his proclamation of the truth, but his commitment to nonviolence—obedience to God, in his eyes—led to eternal liberation in the resurrection. The cross is not a sign of defeat. Rather, it is the symbol for the victory Jesus won by nonviolence. His followers, as described in the book of Acts, slowly came to realize in their own lives the radical truth of this new way, and St. Paul, the foremost spokesperson of the early community, sought eagerly to tell the whole world of this new life of nonviolent love lived in Jesus the Christ. Finally, the book of Revelation, written by an exiled Christian in an age of persecution and fidelity, envisions eternal life for all those who followed the nonviolent, loving, illegal, unreformable Jesus. Those followers gave their blood for God's kingdom, in keeping with the "Way." Such a willingness, we are told, is a tenet of our faith lives. These scripture stories and truths are the narratives that can renew the Christian story of nonviolent resistance in our own lives and time for Christians all around the world, including here in the United States.

The Hebrew Scriptures Through the Prophetic Eyes of Peace

The fulfillment of the Hebrew scriptures that Jesus brings is the good news that the God of liberation and justice portrayed in the Hebrew Bible—the God of Exodus, the God who liberates those held in bondage, the God of the Psalms and prophets—is actually a God of nonviolence who resists injustice through suffering rather than killing, overcomes death by dying and then rising, and saves the powerless through the power of nonviolent love. The evangelists deliberately describe Jesus referring to the Hebrew Bible to support his actions, yet more and more they put Jesus in the specific tradition of the prophets and their word. They portray Jesus as a humble messiah determined to liberate people into a new creation of justice and peace. From Isaiah to Jeremiah to Daniel, the prophets of justice and peace are invoked as his story is told.[3]

Jesus, as a devout Jew, surely would have known the Psalms well. He would have worshiped the God of the psalmist as the God "who saves the upright of heart" (Psalm 7), "the defense of the fatherless and the oppressed" (Psalm 10), the One who has "compassion" and "kindness from of old," "who guides the humble to justice" (Psalm 25), the One who "loves justice and right" (Psalm 33), the Lord who "is close to the brokenhearted" (Psalm 34), the One who has "pity for the lowly and the poor, who saves the lives of the poor, who redeems them from fraud and violence" (cf. Psalm 72). Our God "is merciful and gracious, slow to anger and abounding in steadfast love and faithfulness," writes the psalmist (86:15, RSV). "Give thanks to [God] for [God] is good; [God's] steadfast love endures forever," the scriptures proclaim in

Psalms 118 and 136 (RSV). Put not your trust in princes, the psalmist warns, but trust in the God who made heaven and earth, who keeps faith forever, secures justice for the oppressed, gives food to the hungry, sets captives free, gives sight to the blind, raises up those that were bowed down, loves the just, protects the strangers, sustains the fatherless and the widow, and thwarts the way of the wicked. From the Gospels, we can conclude that Jesus steadfastly worshiped this God who does justice. Like every devout Jew, Jesus worshiped the God of the Psalms.

But though the psalmist describes God as "compassionate" and "merciful," on occasion he implores the wrath of God on his enemies, fully expecting God to murder the people whom the psalmist does not like. "Have no pity on any worthless traitors," we read in Psalm 59. "O God, slay them, lest they beguile my people. . . . Consume them in wrath; consume, till they are no more" (Ps. 59:6, 12, 14). After such an enthusiastic prayer for God to do violence, the writer of this psalm then continues, "I will sing of your strength and revel at dawn in your kindness" (v. 17).

The implication underlying many of these verses is that God will hear these prayers and quickly crush these opponents in the most violent of manners. Christians and Jews alike for centuries have used the underlying assumptions of these prayers to justify all sorts of violence, indeed, every war in modern history. Yet devout Jews like Jesus who understood the goodness of God read these Psalms through the eyes of the prophets, in a vision of a God who hungers to liberate the oppressed and reconcile *all* people without destroying anyone.

From his understanding of Hebrew scriptures, and in answer to the prophetic call for justice, Jesus goes further and reveals God as a God who does indeed support justice for the oppressed, but through active nonviolence, not violent retribution. Jesus worships the God of love and calls on God who is nonviolent to protect him, and to help him love his enemies, indeed, to forgive those who will kill him. Like the psalmist, Jesus asks, "O Lord, . . . who shall dwell on your holy hill?" and with his life's message, agrees with the answer—the one "who walks blamelessly and does what is right; who speaks truth from his [her] heart; who does not slander with his [her] tongue, and does no evil to his [her] friend, nor takes up a reproach against his [her] neighbor" (Ps. 15:1–3, RSV). Jesus would have prayed, "Your kindness reaches to heaven; your faithfulness, to the clouds. . . . How precious is your kindness, O God! . . . Keep up your kindness toward your friends, your just defense of the upright of heart" (Ps. 36:6, 8, 11). Instead of believing the implication that God might willfully strike down anyone, Jesus affirms the image of God as one who wants to build up everyone and reconcile everyone with everyone else. Jesus affirms a God of life who loves life and resists death without harming anyone.

The evangelists make a point of characterizing Jesus as one who chooses to fulfill the prophet's call for nonviolence and resistance. Isaiah's words are particularly important to their understanding of Jesus.[4] According to the evangelists, Jesus took the second half of the book of Isaiah, which modern scholars commonly call "Second Isaiah," as a guiding image, and sought to fulfill that image of a nonviolent messiah who resisted the powers of death through suffering love and service. Jesus used Isaiah's model of the *ebed yahweh* or "suffering servant of God." Jesus embraces Isaiah's vision of a weaponless, nonviolent kingdom, where the lamb shall lie down with the lion, where there is no violence and no fear. He hears the cry of God, who says, "Fear not, I am with you; be not dismayed; I am your God. I will strengthen you, and help you, and uphold you with my right hand of justice" (Isa. 41:10). The God of liberation portrayed in Isaiah says, "Fear not, for I have redeemed you: I have called you by name: you are mine" (Isa. 43:1). Isaiah's God, a God of justice, wants people to love justice by living nonviolently and serving one another. "How beautiful upon the mountains are the feet of him who brings glad tidings, announcing peace, bearing good news . . . " the prophet writes (Isa. 52:7).

Seek [God] while [God] may be found, call upon [God] while [God] is near; let the wicked forsake his [her] way, and the unrighteous [person] his [her] thoughts; let him [her] return to [God] that [God] may have mercy on him [her], and to our God, for [God] will abundantly pardon. For my thoughts are not your thoughts, neither are your ways my ways, says God. (Isa. 55:6–8, RSV)

When Jesus appears in the beginning of the Gospel of Luke, to begin his public ministry in the synagogue at Nazareth, he turns to the prophetic word of Isaiah. Jesus finds a passage that he announces "is fulfilled" in the audience's hearing. The passage comes amidst the description of the *ebed Yahweh,* the portrait of the messiah not as a military leader or political victor wielding power through violence over his enemies, but a messiah founded in lowliness and a determination to do what is just, the object of torture, scorn, humiliation, and capital punishment. Luke paints a portrait of Jesus turning to the chapters in the book of Isaiah on nonviolence and resistance, and there, reading aloud his mission of redemption, a mission rooted in nonviolent love:

The spirit of God is upon me, because [God] has anointed me to bring good tidings to the afflicted; [God] has sent me to bind up the brokenhearted, to proclaim liberty to the captives, and the opening of the prison to those who are bound; to proclaim the year of [God's] favor. (Isa. 61:1–2, RSV)

Jesus identifies with the nonviolent love of God. He will be a messiah of nonviolent love, worshiping, honoring, and speaking for the God who, up to this point, has been so misunderstood in human history. God's name had long been maligned; because of the human proclivity to respond with violence in all its forms, humans long assumed that God was a God of violence. Jesus begins his public work with the scandalous, radical, earth-shaking news: Our God is nonviolent and is liberating us all, beginning with the poor and oppressed, from our addiction to violence and death.[5]

The Sermon on the Mount: A Guide to Nonviolent Resistance

The Sermon on the Mount, written by the evangelist Matthew, was a social and political declaration of nonviolence and resistance to evil.[6] Written as the political platform for Jesus' campaign of nonviolent revolution, it begins, like Buddha's noble eightfold path, with eight steps in the life of nonviolent resistance. First, Jesus' sermon on nonviolent resistance declares that nonviolence begins in the solitude of one's heart and soul, in life among the materially poor and op-pressed:

Blessed are the poor in spirit; for theirs is the kingdom of heaven. (Matt. 5:3)

From a heart of nonviolent love—the poor in spirit, the ground zero of emptiness—compassion and resistance proceed:

Blessed are they who mourn; they shall be comforted.
Blessed are the meek; for they will inherit the land.
Blessed are they who hunger and thirst for justice; for they will be satisfied.
Blessed are the merciful; for they will be shown mercy.
Blessed are the clean of heart; for they will see God.
Blessed are the peacemakers; they will be called children of God.
Blessed are they who are persecuted for justice's sake; for theirs is the kingdom of heaven.
Blessed are you when they insult you and persecute you and utter every kind of evil against you [falsely] because of me. Rejoice and be glad, for your reward will be great in heaven. Thus they persecuted the prophets who were before you. (Matt. 5:4–12)

The evangelist puts these eight progressive steps of nonviolence and resistance in deliberate order, but is careful to state that the means of resistance and the end of resistance are the same: the kingdom of God is the practice of nonviolent love on earth. Those who are poor in spirit or nonviolent of heart are blessed, for the kingdom of God is theirs, now, in their hearts. As they proceed to live the life of truth and compassion, they eventually will be persecuted (and killed) but the kingdom of God—God's reign of love and truth and justice—will remain with them. That, indeed, is cause for rejoicing.

Matthew's manifesto for radical discipleship through active nonviolence actually begins with a description of the life of Jesus himself, nonviolent resister par excellence. As an itinerant preacher and experimenter in truth, Jesus walked the steps of the beatitudes. He could explain them because he lived them, died for them, and lives again in them. From his perspective of revolutionary faith, he understood what a true blessing from God would be, and spoke from his experience.

The six antitheses of Matthew's text of the Sermon on the Mount revolve around a nonviolent way of life, with love and truth at the

33

center. Not only is killing outlawed in this kingdom of nonviolent love, but any thought of killing, any anger in one's heart, any violence in one's being is a violation of nonviolence. Reconciliation with all human beings is the key to nonviolence. A peaceable spirit is to be sought and maintained; nonviolence of the heart and in practice is essential.

Matthew's points on nonviolence culminate with the central themes of active resistance to the forces of evil and the love of enemies. Unfortunately, various translators of these texts, if not distorting the message, have used language that has confused readers for centuries. In *Violence and Nonviolence in South Africa: Jesus' Third Way,* Walter Wink deals precisely with this confusion and the problem of language as it effects these central themes of Jesus' sermon. "When given a fair hearing in its original social context," Wink declares, "[Jesus' teaching in the Sermon on the Mount] is arguably one of the most revolutionary political statements ever uttered."[7]

Offer no resistance to one who is evil. When someone strikes you on [your] right cheek, turn the other one to him as well. If anyone wants to go to law with you over your tunic, hand him your cloak as well. Should anyone press you into service for one mile, go with him for two miles. Give to the one who asks of you, and do not turn your back on one who wants to borrow. (Matt. 5:39–41)

Jesus' nonresistance is in truth the law of noncooperation with evil, the practice of nonviolent love with others. When Matthew writes that we should offer no resistance, he means that we should offer *no violent resistance,* such as the methods of the Zealots and just-war revolutionaries. As Wink explains,

The Greek word [for "no resistance"—*antistenai*] is made up of two parts: *anti,* a word still used in English for "against," and *histemi,* a verb which in its noun form *(stasis)* means violent rebellion, armed revolt, sharp dissension. . . . The term generally refers to a potentially lethal disturbance or armed revolution. A proper translation of Jesus' teaching would then be, 'Do not strike back at evil (or one who has done you evil) in kind. Do not give blow for blow. Do not retaliate against violence with violence.' Jesus was no less committed to opposing evil than the anti-Roman resistance fighters. The only difference was over the means to be used: *how* one should fight evil.[8]

Jesus says that when violence is done to a person, do not cooperate with that violence by continuing the spirit of violence. Do not respond in turn with violence, but do respond with action that will change the situation. Resistance for Jesus could not be a violent resistance. Rather, his resistance was through creative nonviolence. Jesus' preaching may at first appear to advocate passivity in the presence of a violent aggressor, but actually it is the most radical form of resistance. It stops violence in its tracks and redirects it onto the path of reconciliation and community building. By looking the aggressor in the eye with love and respect, the noncooperator seeks to win the person over to friendship and love. This is the essence of redemption. Jesus' words call for total noncooperation with violence. Rejecting passivity and violent resistance, Jesus proposes a third way: nonviolent resistance for the sake of justice and peace.

Jesus' three examples of such resistance (Matt. 5:38–41), seen in their true context, propose radical reactions to oppression. In the first instance, the Gospel specifically speaks of being struck on the right cheek and advocates turning the other. The only way one could strike the right cheek with the right hand would have been with the back of the hand. As Wink points out, Jesus' example refers to an insult, when someone is humiliated with a backhand slap, as opposed to being beaten with the full force of someone's fist. "Turning the other cheek" in the face of this humiliation then would rob the oppressor of the power to humiliate, and, in effect, disarm the oppressor.[9]

Jesus was showing one way to wear down our adversaries and those who use violence to the point at which they give up their violence, recognize our common humanity, and are transformed by the love we bear them. He speaks nothing less than pure revolution, a completely new and different response to the world of violence. The attitude of one who turns the other cheek and does not strike back is otherworldly, indicative of a person whose very being is rooted not in the world of violence but in a world of love and peacefulness. Jesus' call to "turn the other cheek" is not a call to passivity but to dynamic, active, nonviolent love. Rather than endure injustice passively, he enjoins us to demonstrate provocatively our resistance to violence. He does not say ignore it, do nothing, but commands something active and positive: turn the other cheek. This turning is a provocative invitation to metanoia, a conversion of heart. It says, Violence has no control over me; come with me into the world of nonviolent love. In turning the other cheek to someone who has struck us, we are indeed protesting with the deepest love and truth that person's violence and inviting him or her to change from the way of violence to the way of love and peace. In commanding us to refuse to run and refuse to strike back, Jesus asks us to show precisely how much we love those who would hurt us, and precisely how far we are willing to go so that we might all be reconciled into the beloved community. Finally, in commanding us to turn the other cheek, Jesus asks us to be willing to show our trust in God and our basic trust in humanity's goodness, to demonstrate that God's Spirit of love will then intercede and reveal to the person his or her act of violence and oppression so that person's sinfulness will cease.

Jesus' second example speaks to the practice, common in his time, of suing poor people for their outer garment because of a debt owed. Roman policy led to widespread indebtedness, and typically only the poorest of the poor would have nothing but an outer garment to give as collateral for a loan.[10] Yet when Jesus urges his listeners to offer up their inner garments as well—and thus to stand completely naked before the court of law—he is challenging the oppressed of the empire to respond creatively, to disarm their opponents. "Nakedness was taboo in Judaism, and shame fell not on the naked party, but on the person viewing or causing one's nakedness (Gen. 9:20–27)," notes Wink. Thus, people would hear about the incident, the lawsuit of the oppressor would be exposed and the injustice uncovered, causing the oppressor to repent.[11]

Jesus' third example, a behest to go two miles with someone rather than just one, referred to the practice of Roman soldiers forcing the poor to carry the soldiers' packs for them. Although the soldiers by law were not to force the people to walk more than one mile for them, the local people felt the weight and pain of political oppression. Jesus' suggestion turns the tables on Roman superiority and demonstrates to the soldier that the oppressed person is a human being with dignity and control over his or her life. He was not attempting to exact revenge or inflict humiliation, but to uncover the common human bonding between the oppressor and the oppressed, so that the soldier would see his mistake and stop oppressing people.[12]

After these admonitions, Jesus commends his listeners to go beyond nationality, to practice a public love for all human beings: "I say to you . . . love your enemies, pray for those who persecute you" (Matt. 5:44). This command to practice nonviolent love with one's enemies, as discussed in chapter 1, is the centerpiece of the sermon. "Go beyond the boundaries of civil love to the radical love that embraces your enemies, even those who would kill you," Jesus commends. When our love goes beyond national boundaries and we choose to be reconciled with all people, then, Jesus says, we will be like God for this is how God acts: God loves God's enemies. God is nonviolent; God loves *everyone*. Do this, Jesus says, so

that you may be sons [daughters] of your Father [Mother] who is in heaven; for [God] makes [God's] sun rise on the evil and on the good, and sends rain on the just and on the unjust. For if you love those who love you, what reward have you? Do not even the tax collectors do the same? And if you salute only your [brothers and sisters], what more are you doing than others? Do not even the Gentiles do the same? You, therefore, must be perfect, as your heavenly Father [Mother] is perfect. (Matt. 5:45–48, RSV)

At this climactic point in the sermon, Jesus points out that God goes beyond national boundaries and loves all people, including the enemies and marginalized peoples of every nation. When Jesus asks us to go beyond the conventional love of civil society to love our enemies and those we would never consider loving, he reveals the very essence of the Divine.

The old adage, "Love your countrymen, but hate your enemy," is not the love God desires, according to Jesus. The *agape* of Jesus' command breaks through civility, pagan practice, and all worldly expectations. Such love is Godly. "Be like God," he commands. "Be perfect," which translates, "Be compassionate: love your enemies." God loves human beings in this very manner. God loves God's enemies and does them good and lends to them without any hope of return. God is kind to the ungrateful and the unjust. When we act this way, we act like God; indeed, Jesus goes so far as to proclaim that we are the daughters and sons of God when we love our enemies. He could not use stronger language to tell us how we could be like God, and just who God is.

Jesus spent his life crossing boundaries, walking across borders, and reconciling divided parties. After presenting the consistent points of this radical nonviolent love in his sermon, and commending his listeners to put the teaching into practice to enable them to live freely, Jesus cured a leper. He healed an ostracized member of society by touching him, an act that would have instantly stigmatized and marginalized Jesus. He put his teaching into practice. He healed a poor person with his nonviolent love and thus resisted society's injustice.

The Gospel of Mark: Jesus' Campaign of Nonviolent Resistance

Ched Myers's reading of the Gospel of Mark outlines and discusses the story of Jesus as a deliberate *campaign* of active nonviolence and resistance, peppered with illegal activity, that built to a climax of nonviolent confrontation with the powers, a confrontation that would most certainly lead to death, but ended with a surprise.[13] Jesus' first public ministry was a direct action campaign, an assault on the Jewish social order in Capernaum. Jesus challenged the symbolic space of the synagogue and attacked the purity code (in the healing of the leper), the debt system (in the healing of a paralytic), and pharisaic privilege. That first campaign concluded with an act of civil disobedience—eating grain in an open field.

Myers's insightful reading sheds light on the episodes when the disciples cross the Sea of Galilee during the storm. He interprets these two Markan episodes (Mark 4:35–41; 6:45–53) as parables of racial reconciliation between the Jew and Gentile sides of the sea. Peacemaking, we begin to see, means crossing treacherous, fearsome waters, from one side to the other and back. It will be like walking on water, a task the disciples can do if only they have faith and overcome their fears. Those episodes become paradigms for the Christian way of life.[14]

Myers continues with a sermon on revolutionary patience, and Jesus' construction of a new social order (in the "miracle cycle," Mark 4:36—

8:9). After the execution of John, the second half of Mark begins with a new prologue and a new call to discipleship with the question, "Who do you say that I am?" Then, a second teaching cycle offers a catechism on nonviolence and detailed points on the new social order, regarding family practice, economic power and community life, and community leadership through servanthood. The second direct action campaign takes Jesus into Jerusalem where he confronts the temple, the place of imperial, political, and religious authority, and thus oppression. After a second sermon on revolutionary patience, Jesus is arrested, tried, and executed.

The Jesus of the Gospels is a nonviolent phenomenon, resisting every unjust and unfair practice and thought of his time. He breaks through social barriers to reach out to those most persecuted and frees them while, at the same time, he speaks out against the oppression of the ruling class in temple and state and invites those rulers to a conversion of heart.[15] Jesus practices civil disobedience—in the broad sense of confronting division and oppression, risking his life in the process—at every turn. He does this with a great sense of obedience to God and a spirit of love toward all.

The Gospels cite numerous instances when Jesus was in trouble for what he had said and done, more than forty times when Jesus was being watched or sought after, and more than twenty-five references to plots against him and his friends.[16] At one point in the Gospel of John (7:19–20), Jesus is accused of being "paranoid," thinking that people are out to get him. The Gospels do show that, in fact, people *were* out to arrest him or throw him off a cliff or kill him. Jesus was in trouble for telling the truth, publicly, for all to hear. He was also in trouble for acting in the truth and for the public uncovering of truth through symbolic action.

When Jesus puts the question to his disciples, "Who do you say that I am?" it is Peter who responds, "The messiah of God." Each of the Synoptic Gospels is quick to explain what this messiahship means: a life of nonviolent resistance that will result in scandal and suffering, arrest and public execution (Mark 8:27—9:1; Matt. 16:13–28; Luke 9:18–27). The Human One [as Myers translates the archaic phrase,

"Son of Man"] "must first suffer greatly and be rejected by the elders, the chief priests, and the scribes, and be killed and on the third day be raised" (Luke 9:22).[17] Jesus' punishment for his provocative challenge was standard for all political revolutionaries: capital punishment. By suffering through love while insisting on justice, Jesus would be the obedient servant of God, the Messiah. The disciples, however, beginning with Peter, did not truly understand this until after his death. As Myers points out, the women who lurk in the background of the Gospel narrative emerge finally as the true disciples, faithful to Jesus even through his brutal execution and the politically risky step of visiting his tomb.[18] Such fidelity results in the news of Jesus' resurrection.

Luke, elaborating on Mark's script, places the dialogue concerning Jesus' identity as a prelude to his decision to face Jerusalem—the scene of his final dramatic act of resistance—and begin the walk to the scene of his "crime." Mark and Matthew point out that Peter challenges Jesus on Jesus' willingness to go to Jerusalem and risk execution. Jesus' rebuke of Peter reveals that Peter's confession of Jesus as the "Messiah" was based on an incorrect, though popular, notion of the coming "Messiah." Most Jews, including the disciples, hoped for the coming of an imperial messiah, a warlike leader who would overcome the Romans in a military battle. Much to the shock of the disciples, Jesus embraces Isaiah's image of a nonviolent, humble messiah who suffers for justice' sake.

In an effort to teach his followers again the nonviolent nature of his public and spiritual resistance, Jesus elucidates the conditions of discipleship:

If any [person] would come after me, let him [her] deny himself [herself] and take up his [her] cross daily and follow me. For whoever would save his [her] life, will lose it; and whoever loses his [her] life for my sake, he [she] will save it. (Luke 9:23–24, RSV)

Jesus states explicitly, in radical language that would have been clearly understood at that time, that discipleship will mean radical love, the loving disobedience that Jesus would manifest, risking pain, scandal, capital punishment. Discipleship to Christ, the *ebed Yahweh,* will mean nonviolent resistance to imperial and religious violence and injustice, regardless of the consequences.

Myers believes that the account of Jesus' transfiguration (Luke 9:28–36) is not the story of Moses and Elijah appearing to Jesus to express their sorrow about his upcoming activity. Rather, the evangelists understand this story to be an affirmation of Jesus' way of nonviolent resistance that embraces suffering through love and becomes redemptive.[19] Although Jesus explains his upcoming campaign of nonviolent civil disobedience, his method of enacting his divine obedience to God the creator, an obedience that would lead to his death, the disciples do not understand the logic of crucifixion, the logic of Jesus' loving nonviolent resistance (Luke 9:43–45). The heart of his message, his way of life, is nearly incomprehensible to his audience, and, as the evangelists suspect, to the reader as well.

In Luke 9:46–48, Jesus confronts the egotism of his followers: become childlike, he commends. He explains the ground zero of his *kenosis* within the context of his teachings of nonviolence. Finally, Luke sets Jesus "firmly resolved to proceed toward Jerusalem," via enemy territory, through a Samaritan town where he was unwelcome. Jesus reprimanded the disciples who wanted "to call down fire from heaven" on those inhospitable Samaritans. The disciples were slow to learn the message of Jesus' sermon, the love of enemies that he was practicing right before their eyes.

Jesus entered Jerusalem using the symbolic tactic of street theater, assuming the disposition of humility by riding on a mule. In Jerusalem, he went to the temple, first to observe, then to disrupt the false worship of that institution, including its profit system. His civil disobedience disrupts the business of making money under a religious guise. Immediately, the ruling authorities plan his death.

Clearly, the nonviolent assault on the temple is the primary *act* of the Jesus narratives. Everything in the story aims toward that encounter between Jesus and the religious/military/imperial complex of his day. It is important to note that this act is definitely nonviolent. Jesus does not hurt anyone; he does not kill anyone; he does not physically mistreat anyone. He *does* disrupt the lives of many people for a short time. He is active and provocative but not harmful. Unfortunately, readers of the

Gospel down through the centuries have interpreted this central story as an act of violence, and have justified every form of murder, including the mass murder of war, in the name of Jesus.

As Myers explains, "Jesus attacks the temple institutions because of the way they exploit the poor."[20] Mark describes Jesus "driving out" all those who bought and sold (Mark 10:15)—an expression that fits within the pivotal parable of the strong man, where a stronger person must bind a strong man in order to plunder his house. Jesus is finally revealed in the temple action as the stronger person plundering the house of this world.

The temple was fundamentally an economic institution that dominated the life of Jerusalem.[21] What Jesus confronts is precisely the ruling-class interests—rooted in the religious elite—who control all commerce and keep the poor under their control. The temple, with its religious cult, has seduced the poor of the region into paying high prices to worship God in the temple. "Mark is not concerned with advocating lower prices for the poor or fair economic practices," Myers notes. "Jesus calls for an end to the entire cultic system—symbolized by his 'overturning' (*katestrepsen*, which can also mean to 'destroy') of the stations" used by the groups in control.[22] Jesus then shuts down the temple altogether. He "forbade anyone to carry any goods (*skeuos*, here meaning any vessel or item needed for the cult) through the temple."[23] Myers writes,

This action suggests some kind of barricade or "guerrilla ban" on all further activities for that day. The point is not to try to speculate on *how* Jesus might have actually accomplished this so much as to understand the *legitimation* such a narrative lends to the practice of [nonviolent] direct action.[24]

Jesus declared that he came to reconstitute the temple as a house of prayer, instead of the den of thieves it had become, a place where the poor were robbed. He told his disciples to abandon their faith in the God of the temple, to repudiate the entire temple system, and to believe solely in the God of love and justice. Jesus speaks of a new "site" for prayer now that the "house of prayer"—the temple—has been abandoned. Myers explains,

This new site is neither geographical nor institutional but ethical: the difficult but imperative practice of mutual forgiveness within the community. As the discipleship catechism stressed, inequality can be prevented only by a living practice of reconciliation and the renunciation of power and privilege. The community's practice of forgiveness becomes the replacement of the redemptive/symbolic system of debt represented in the temple. The community becomes truly the "priesthood of all believers," the place of prayer "for all peoples."[25]

Jesus has been deliberately provocative; his resistance has been active, public, and disruptive. When he is arrested, and eventually put through a mock trial, he is charged with being an agitator and disturber of the peace: "We found this man misleading our people; he opposes the paying of taxes to Caesar, and maintains that he is the Messiah, a king" (Luke 23:2).

Arrested at night, secretly tried, abandoned by friends, condemned, tortured, and mocked, Jesus carries the cross to Calvary where he is stripped and nailed to it. Barabbas is released because the people applaud him as a genuine hero and true revolutionary who used violence and was willing to kill a Roman soldier.[26] Jesus' nonviolence is put to the ultimate test. His obedience to God lasted throughout his suffering; he did not strike back or bear ill will to those who attempted to kill him. Rather, he prayed to God, "Forgive them; for they know not what they do" (Luke 23:34, RSV). He maintained a spirit of hope—the spirit of nonviolence—in a world of total darkness and blood. At the moment of death, he whispered, "Into your hands, I commit my spirit" (Luke 23:46, RSV).

Jesus' resistance, his public display of the truth, was rejected, and he was crucified. Jesus maintained the spirit of nonviolence at every moment of the ordeal, and saw the world from the cross through the eyes of nonviolent love. His spirit of love as a consequence of truth-telling redeems humanity, his followers later realized. He is the Human One portrayed by the prophets. On the following Sunday, when the resurrection of Jesus was revealed, when he returned with the gift of his peace, the disciples were overcome with joy and realized, perhaps for the first time, what his life had been about. Obedience to the Father/ Mother of Jesus meant resistance to death through nonviolent love.

Jesus explained the scriptures again, retaught his message of the great sermon, and showered them with affection. With the gift of his spirit at Pentecost, the disciples began their own public journey to the temple and to Calvary. The disciples became nonviolent resisters following in the steps of their master, the crucified one.

The cross, as Myers has written, was "neither religious icon nor metaphor for personal anguish or humility. It has only one meaning: that terrible form of capital punishment reserved by imperial Rome for political dissenters. Thus, discipleship is revealed as a vocation of nonviolent resistance to the powers."[27] Jesus was murdered by crucifixion for suggesting that Roman officials and religious authorities were not the highest authority, but that God is the highest authority and obedience should be reserved for God alone. Imperial power and its religious support are corrupt, violent, and unjust. The nonviolent Jesus gave true authority to God, who, he said, is nonviolent love and justice itself. By suffering death rather than inflicting it, Jesus realized in his own body the full power of nonviolence and became a sign of redemption. Since his resistance and his nonviolence were complete and pure, he proved to the world the height of God's power, the extent of God's authority over all. By plunging into the depth of suffering love, Jesus was given power, later revealed and passed on to the disciples in the spirit of resurrection.

The resurrection signaled the liberation of Jesus' disciples. Myers points out, in particular, the circular nature of the Gospel of Mark— the disciples' mission was to return to Galilee where the discipleship story would begin again. The implication for the reader of Mark's Gospel with its unfinished ending is that the reader is invited to enter into the Gospel story along with the disciples who are returning to Galilee. The resurrection empowered the disciples to take up the cross of nonviolent resistance. The experiences narrated in the Gospel, climaxing in the resurrection, empower readers to take up that same cross. Commenting on the young man who appears in the tomb in Mark's conclusion, Myers writes:

The full revelation of the Human One has resulted in neither triumphal victory for the community (as the disciples had hoped), nor the restored Davidic kingdom (as the rebels had hoped), nor tragic failure

44

and defeat (as the reader had feared). It has resulted in nothing more and nothing less than the regeneration of the messianic mission. If we have eyes to "see" the advent of the Human One we will be able to "see" Jesus still going before us. The "invitation" by Jesus, via the young man, to follow him to Galilee, is the third and last call to discipleship. He evokes both hope and terror. Hope, in that he who once joined in the naked shame of abandonment (14:51f.) now stands in new attire; terror, in that his new clothes are that of a martyr figure. Is the disciple/reader also willing to undergo such a transformation?[28]

Jesus' nonviolent resistance to worldly powers, which culminated in his crucifixion and resurrection, demonstrated that strict obedience to the highest authority—God—is not another form of slavery or bondage. Rather it is the ultimate experience of freedom and paves the way to a new world of justice and love, God's kingdom on earth. It leads through a path of blood to eternal life. Such is the way to justice and true peace for all.

Early Christian Writings: Testimonies on the Nonviolent Christ

The Christian scriptures that follow the Gospels in the Bible were written to encourage a faithful people on the road to discipleship and freedom, the road of nonviolent resistance to worldly violence. The Acts of the Apostles recount this experience of liberation, first realized by the disciples on the day of Pentecost, when they broke out of the upper room—and the fear that kept them there—into the streets to take up the work of nonviolent resistance. Within a short time, they themselves were arrested, hauled before imperial and religious authorities for interrogation, tortured, and killed. These accounts tell of the nonviolent spirit in their hearts which poured from them literally into the streets and into the world. Their resistance was nonviolent; the consequence of their obedience to Jesus was imprisonment.[29] The letters of encouragement by the convert Paul speak of the need to maintain that spirit of nonviolent love, as well as the need to resist the worldly authority that despises God's authority and seeks to undo creation by promoting death. Acts and the letters of Paul demonstrate that the early disciples became a community of nonviolent resistance, and struggled to form such communities of resistance and faith throughout the world.[30]

From prison, Paul wrote that God in fact is a God of nonviolence and resistance, for God raised Christ "from the dead and made him sit at [God's] right hand in the heavenly places, far above all rule and authority and power and dominion, and above every name that is named, not only in this age but also in that which is to come" (Eph. 1:20–21, RSV). God affirmed and vindicated the nonviolent, resisting Jesus, and exulted him to Christhood. Such talk was a profound turnabout for Paul, the notorious murderer who had previously roamed the countryside looking for Christians to arrest. It is easy to forget that Paul stood by and encouraged the stoning of Stephen, the first martyr. Acts takes note of his past so many times (Acts 7:58; 8:3; 9:1–2, 21; 22:3–5, 19–20; 26:9–11) precisely because Paul had learned the lesson of repentance; he had been converted from violence to active nonviolence. He no longer supported murder, but became the prime example of a disciple, spending his days forming communities of active love throughout the Roman Empire. His words reveal his true understanding of Jesus' life and its reconciling power, as this passage from Ephesians shows:

Now in Christ Jesus you who once were far off have been brought near in the blood of Christ. For he is our peace, who has made us both one, and has broken down the dividing wall of hostility, by abolishing in his flesh the law of commandments and ordinances, that he might create in himself one new [hu]man[kind] in place of the two, so making peace, and might reconcile us both to God in one body through the cross, thereby bringing the hostility to an end. And he came and preached peace to you who were far off and peace to those who were near; for through him we both have access in one Spirit to God. (Eph. 2:13–18, RSV)

The conclusion of this letter to the Ephesians is a call to maintain Christ's spirit of nonviolence and resistance to the forces of evil. We are at war, Paul is saying, but our tactic and spirit is militant nonviolence.

Be strong in [God] and in the strength of [God's] might. Put on the whole armor of God, that you may be able to stand against the wiles of the devil. For we are not contending against flesh and blood, but against the principalities, against the powers, against the world rulers of this present darkness, against the spiritual hosts of wickedness in the heavenly places. Therefore take the whole armor of God, that you may be able to withstand in the evil day, and having done all, to stand. Stand therefore, having girded your loins with truth, and having put on the breastplate of righteousness, and having shod your feet with the equipment of the gospel of peace; besides all these, taking the shield of faith, with which you can quench all the flaming darts of the evil one. And take the helmet of salvation, and the sword of the Spirit, which is the word of God. Pray at all times in the Spirit, with all prayer and supplication. To that end keep alert with all perseverance, making supplication for all the saints. (Eph. 6:10–18, RSV)

The armor of God to which Paul refers is the armor of nonviolent love that resists evil. His message is an exhortation to follow the way of the cross, to practice nonviolence and resistance to evil until the end of the world, when the reign of the Spirit of nonviolent love is fully revealed.

To the Philippians, Paul wrote, "Unfortunately, many go about in a way which shows them to be enemies of the cross of Christ. I have often said this to you before; this time I say it with tears. Such as these will end in disaster! . . . As you well know, we have our citizenship in heaven; it is from there that we eagerly await the coming of our Savior, the Lord Jesus Christ" (Phil. 3:18, 20). Paul warns his friends in Thessalonica of the age of lawlessness, that is, the spirit of violence and greed that brings death and destruction (2 Thess. 2:3–10). The spirit of Paul's writings issues forth as a political message of nonviolent resistance rooted in the spiritual depths of Christ's love.

Similarly, other writings such as the first letter of Peter, which was written to Christians in the name of the disciple, explicitly call for resistance rooted in the nonviolence of Christ. Here, the author invokes the underlying call for nonviolent resistance in Psalm 34.

All of you, have unity of spirit, sympathy, love of [brothers and sisters], a tender heart and a humble mind. Do not return evil for evil or reviling for reviling; but on the contrary bless, for to this you have been called, that you may obtain a blessing. For "he [she] that would love life and see good days, let him [her] keep his [her] tongue from evil and his [her] lips from speaking guile; let him [her] turn away from evil and do right; let him [her] seek peace and pursue it. For the eyes of [God] are upon the righteous, and [God's] ears are open to their prayer. But the face of [God] is against those that do evil."

Now who is there to harm you if you are zealous for what is right? But even if you do suffer for righteousness' sake, you will be blessed. Have no fear of them, nor be troubled, but in your hearts reverence Christ as Lord. Always be prepared to make a defense to any one who calls you to account for the hope that is in you, yet do it with gentleness and reverence; and keep your conscience clear, so that, when you are abused, those who revile your good behavior in Christ may be put to shame. For it is better to suffer for doing right, if that should be God's will, than for doing wrong. (1 Pet. 3:8–17, RSV)

Christ suffered in the flesh; therefore, arm yourselves with his same mentality, the writer urges. Such is the road that lies ahead for anyone who takes the name Christian.

The testament of nonviolence written by the early community of nonviolent resisters, the followers of Jesus, urges steadfast obedience to the way of the cross. The Christian scriptures conclude with the vision of the heavenly kingdom where the nonviolent Christ reigns, where all who have lived the truth of nonviolent love find eternal life and joy. The vision of Revelation portrays the battle between violence and nonviolent love, with the power of God in the nonviolent Christ winning eternal life and victory. The book of Revelation is a testament of nonviolent resistance that continues the tradition begun by Jesus of Nazareth.[31] Those who worship in joy are the followers of Jesus, the way, the Lamb of God (an image of nonviolent love). The fulfillment of a life of nonviolent resistance and love is the vision of God's reign, as described in Revelation:

Then I saw a new heaven and a new earth; for the first heaven and the first earth had passed away, and the sea was no more. And I saw the holy city, new Jerusalem, coming down out of heaven from God, prepared as a bride adorned for her husband; and I heard a loud voice from the throne saying, "Behold, the dwelling of God is with [hu]man[kind]. [God] will dwell with them, and they shall be [God's] people, and God will be with them; [God] will wipe away every tear from their eyes, and death shall be no more, neither shall there be mourning nor crying nor pain any more, for the former things have passed away."

And he [she] who sat upon the throne said, "Behold, I make all things new. . . . I am the Alpha and the Omega, the beginning and the end. To the thirsty I will give from the fountain of the water of life without payment. He [she] who conquers shall have this heritage, and I will be his [her] God and he [she] shall be my son [daughter]." (Rev. 21:1–7, RSV)

What the author describes in the vision is what Jesus tried to explain in the Sermon on the Mount: there is a natural law of the spirit. For those who first seek God's kingdom and God's justice (the Spirit of nonviolence, forgiveness, resistance to evil), everything else will be provided—forever. Those who by practicing violence continually reject God's kingdom and God's justice will be caught in the never-ending downward spiral of violence and death. Jesus is explaining the laws of reality, and pleads to all humanity: Love God with all your heart, with all your soul, with all your mind. Love your neighbor as yourself. Do not kill. Do not hurt one another. Resist injustice and death through suffering love; choose life. Enter the kingdom of nonviolent love now and live forever.

Our God Is Nonviolent: The Revelation of Jesus

The story of Jesus reveals the truth that God is nonviolent love; that indeed nonviolent love is God. Jesus invites all to live in the love of nonviolence by resisting death and choosing life, by siding with the poor through liberating acts of peace and justice. Jesus reveals that our God loves all humanity unconditionally. In the revelation of Jesus, we find that our God is completely nonviolent, totally loving. Our God has been nonviolently loving human beings since God created us. Jesus reveals our God to be a suffering God, constantly loving, sacrificing God's self, dying for love of us, suffering the pain and violence we show to God, yet constantly responding to that violence with nonviolent love. This is what Jesus taught and revealed with his life and death and resurrection.

As more people came to see Jesus as the Human One, the fullest revelation of God on earth, our understanding and image of God changed. As German theologian Dorothee Solle writes, we now know God as unarmed love.

49

God does not want to protect himself or keep himself remote. God renounced violence and the kind of intervention that those in power practice. God does not make use of violence. In Jesus Christ, God disarmed himself. God surrendered himself without protection and without arms to those who keep crying for more and more protection and arms. In Jesus Christ, God renounced violence. And of course he did this unilaterally, without waiting for us to lay down our weapons first. In Christ, God disarmed unilaterally. God took the first step. God did not wait for others, insisting that they be the first to lay down their weapons. In Christ, God began unilaterally, on his own side, to renounce the threat of violence.[32]

Our God is compassionate and through Jesus invites us to be compassionate, to be nonviolent. Responding to this invitation, becoming like our nonviolent God who resists and overcomes death through love, brings us liberation and the fullness of life.

Jesus said to his disciples that they would know the truth and the truth would set them free. Then Jesus revealed that he *is* the truth and that the truth of his life—a life of nonviolent resistance, loving disobedience, obedience to the God of life—is a way of liberation. Jesus is known today in the context of North America through the liberating acts of nonviolent resistance, loving disobedience to the imperial, national, and personal laws that inflict injustice and death upon others. By seeking the unarmed, crucified, and risen Christ, Christians seek the transformation, redemption, and salvation of humanity. When we accept the consequences of discipleship to this nonviolent resister—the consequences of crucifixion and resurrection—and continue publicly to seek the truth of justice for all through nonviolent love, and act on this truth and proclaim it publicly in love, then we are truly free.

Notes

1. Ched Myers, *Binding the Strong Man: A Political Reading of Mark's Story of Jesus* (Maryknoll, N.Y.: Orbis Books, 1988), 13, 31.

2. See, e.g., John Howard Yoder, *The Politics of Jesus* (Grand Rapids: Wm. B. Eerdmans, 1972); Andre Trocme, *Jesus and the Nonviolent Revolution* (Scottdale, Pa.: Herald Press, 1973); Walter Wink, *Violence and Nonviolence in South Africa: Jesus' Third Way* (Philadelphia: New Society Pub., 1987); Willard

Swartley, *Slavery, Sabbath, War and Women* (Scottdale: Pa.: Herald Press, 1983); Richard Taylor and Ronald Sider, *Nuclear Holocaust and Christian Hope* (Downers Grove, Il.: Intervarsity, 1982); and Richard McSorley, *New Testament Basis for Peacemaking* (Scottdale, Pa.: Herald Press, 1985).

3. Myers, *Binding the Strong Man*, 97–99. See also McSorley, *New Testament Basis for Peacemaking*, chap. 2: "But Doesn't the Old Testament Allow Killing?" 53–67; and Swartley, *Slavery, Sabbath, War and Women*, chap. 3: "The Bible and War," 96–149.

4. See Myers, *Binding the Strong Man*, on Isaiah, 124–27, 173, 302, 309, 363, 378.

5. See Trocme, *Jesus and the Nonviolent Revolution*, 19-76; and Yoder, *The Politics of Jesus*, 34–40, 64–77.

6. See Segundo Galilea, *The Beatitudes* (Maryknoll, N.Y.: Orbis Books, 1985).

7. Walter Wink, *Violence and Nonviolence in South Africa: Jesus' Third Way* (Philadelphia: New Society Pub., 1987), 12–34.

8. Ibid., 13.

9. Ibid., 16.

10. Ibid., 17.

11. Ibid., 18–19.

12. Ibid., 20–22.

13. Myers, *Binding the Strong Man*, 137–407.

14. Ibid., 194–97.

15. Ibid., 436–37. See also the following chapters in Jim Wallis, *The Rise of Christian Conscience* (San Francisco: Harper & Row, 1987): Ched Myers, "By What Authority? The Bible and Civil Disobedience," 237–46; Richard Taylor, "With All Due Respect: A Historical Perspective on Civil Disobedience," 247–55; and Bill Kellermann, "The Cleansing of the Temple: Jesus and Symbolic Action," 256–61.

16. Bill Kellermann, "Examining Jesus' Response to Surveillance," *Sojourners*, February, 1986.

17. Myers, *Binding the Strong Man*, 37.

18. Ibid., 396–97.

19. Ibid., 249–56.

20. Ibid., 299–301. See also Kellermann, "Cleansing of the Temple" in Wallis, *Rise of Christian Conscience*, 256–61.

21. Myers, *Binding the Strong Man*, 300.

22. Ibid., 301.

23. Ibid.

24. Ibid., 302.

25. Ibid., 306.

26. Ibid., 296, 380–81.

27. Ched Myers, "Embracing the Way of Jesus: A Catechism of the Cross," *Sojourners* (August/September 1987): 27.

28. Myers, *Binding the Strong Man*, 399.

29. See Rick Cassidy, *Politics and Society in the Acts of the Apostles* (Maryknoll, N.Y.: Orbis Books, 1987).

30. See Rick Cassidy, *Politics and Society in the Acts of the Apostles* (Maryknoll, N.Y.: Orbis Books, 1987); and Richard McSorley, *New Testament Basis for Peacemaking* (Scottdale, Pa.: Herald Press, 1985).

31. See Daniel Berrigan, *The Nightmare of God* (Portland, Oreg.: Sunburst Press, 1983); and Allan Boesak, *Comfort and Protest: Reflections on the Apocalypse of John of Patmos* (Philadelphia: Westminster Press, 1987).

32. Dorothee Solle, *Of War and Love* (Maryknoll, N.Y.: Orbis Books, 1981), 96–97.

3

Following Jesus in the Nuclear Age

THE LESSONS OF GANDHI

Mohandas Gandhi's assassination on January 30, 1948, occurred at a watershed in history—shortly after the end of World War II, after the atomic bombings of Hiroshima and Nagasaki, after India's independence and civil war. He died still passionately committed to his message of nonviolence. A Hindu, he captured his nation's heart with his zeal for peace and justice. In the process, he caused many Christians to take a new look at their own gospel and calling.

Over forty years later, the cost of the nuclear arms race has soared to unimaginable numbers. Millions of dollars are spent each day on weapons ($1.7 million per minute), while more than forty-five thousand people will die of starvation that same day. In Gandhi's own country, nonviolence and resistance to evil are now rarely practiced. Indeed, the world has moved far from his teachings.

What has become of Gandhi's experiments in truth, his rediscovery and application of nonviolence as the personal and public method for positive social change? What can his nonviolent resistance and truth-force mean for people in the U.S. today? Such questions are worth pondering. The answers may help us create a world without war.

Gandhi never achieved political office. He sought solidarity with the poorest of the poor and in this powerlessness found the power of love and truth. "My message is my life," he wrote, and his life was a never-ending series of experiments in truth and nonviolence. Through his steadfast faith and regular prayerful meditation on the Bhagavad Gita and the Sermon on the Mount, he was able to move mountains. His religious search led to an insight into the underlying truth of nonviolence in Hinduism and in Christianity, in Eastern and Western religious traditions. Gandhi reversed the Western concept of God that says God is truth, to Truth is God, and in so doing he found a way to liberation and resistance, the way of nonviolence. He saw nonviolence as the compassionate love of God in action.

Nonviolence was never simply a tactic for Gandhi but a way of life, a matter of the heart, as we discussed in chapter 1. From his inner unity, achieved through years of discipline and renunciation, Gandhi found the ability to suffer for justice' sake, to refuse to harm others, to accept imprisonment for the sake of peace. For his friends in the independence movement, he wrote an essay, "How to Enjoy Jail." Such an essay was the fruit of an inner freedom already realized. Gandhi's nonviolence starts from within and moves outward. It leads to heartfelt joy found when one is jailed for a just cause.

His willingness to lay down his life for suffering humanity created new life in himself and in those around him. Through careful study and discipline, he explored deeply the practice of truth, and his discoveries were open to all. "I have not the shadow of a doubt that any man or woman can achieve what I have, if he or she would make the same effort and cultivate the same hope and faith."[1]

Gandhi's experimentation in truth continued to the last day of his life. He constantly sought new ways to pursue the truth of nonviolence in his own heart and therefore in his world. We in the the United States have much to learn from Gandhi's experiments. As we race ahead madly toward and with violence, his message of nonviolence waits calmly to be heard and undertaken anew.

Belief in God as the truth and the practice of that belief through a life of active nonviolence were the essence of Gandhi's thinking. Gandhi took belief in God seriously. "What I want to achieve, what I have been striving and pining to achieve these thirty years," he wrote in his autobiography, "is self-realization, to see God face to face. I live and move and have my being in pursuit of this goal. All that I do by way of speaking and writing, and all my ventures in the political field, are directed to this same end."[2] Gandhi saw the face of God in the poorest peasant and in the public struggle of nonviolent resistance and love. He sought to uncover truth at every turn and found that justice and nonviolence were at the heart of that journey in truth. "You may be sent to the gallows, or put to torture, but if you have Truth in you, you will experience an inner joy."[3]

One cannot seek truth, Gandhi discovered, and still continue to participate in violence and injustice either by holding them within one's heart or by inflicting them on the world. Truthseekers, he maintained, will soon discover the wisdom of nonviolence and commit themselves to that way of life. Nonviolence is the power of the powerless, Gandhi believed. It is also the power of God, the only power that overcomes evil, including the evil of the bomb. "Nonviolence is the greatest and most active force in the world. . . . One person who can express nonviolence in life exercises a force superior to all the forces of brutality. . . . Nonviolence cannot be preached. It has to be practiced," he insisted. "If we remain nonviolent, hatred will die as everything does, from disuse."[4]

Gandhi's nonviolence began with prayer, solitude, and fasting. He discovered that by avoiding power in all its forms of violence and control and by renouncing the desire for immediate results, a person would be reduced to zero. All ambitions, personal goals, and egotistic desires would be renounced, and the Spirit of God would be freer to move in one's heart, in one's actions, and thus in the world. From this ground zero of emptiness, the compassionate love of God—nonviolence—can grow like a mustard plant and spread like wildfire. At this point, Gandhi wrote, the individual becomes "irresistible" to others who see the truth anew. The spiritual, actual effect of one's action and nonviolence becomes "all-pervasive," catching on like fire in the hearts of people. "This comes when a person reduces herself to zero," Gandhi insisted.[5] The deeper one goes into this self-emptiness (Christian scriptures call it *kenosis* and St. John of the Cross called it "the dark night of the soul"), the more wide-ranging the reach of one's nonviolent love, even to the point of changing the world, as Jesus' life did and Gandhi tried to do.

Gandhi's experiments in truth revealed that the mandate of the Sermon on the Mount—the love of one's enemies—is of critical importance. Throughout Gandhi's public trials of nonviolence, he manifested a desire for reconciliation and friendship with his opponents. Just as he befriended General Smuts in South Africa, Gandhi struggled to win over Jinnah, his Muslim opponent in India, through nonviolent love. His satyagraha campaigns began in a community of love and resistance and he endeavored to extend that beloved community as far and as wide as possible. When in prison, Gandhi befriended his jailers.

Gandhi believed that one must dissociate the self from every form of evil, and his noncooperation campaigns put into public practice the teachings of Jesus. His willingness to suffer for justice' sake and his apparent cooperation with violence actually were noncooperation with violence. The violence ended there, in Gandhi's own person, as it had ended also in Jesus, and Gandhi's noncooperation with evil, his nonviolent resistance, led to the presence of new life and love.

Gandhi confessed, "I learnt the lesson of nonviolence from my wife [Kasturbai], when I tried to bend her to my will. Her determined resistance to my will, on the one hand, and her quiet submission to the suffering my stupidity involved, on the other, ultimately made me ashamed of myself and cured me of my stupidity."[6] Kasturbai taught Mohandas that nonviolence naturally includes feminism, the practice of the equality of the sexes. Gandhi became an advocate of women's rights and maintained that if the world was to make any progress, sexism must be banned and forgotten.

Gandhi always tried to stand with the outcasts of society and to speak for the rights of the marginalized. In India, such solidarity meant taking a radical, scandalizing public stand on behalf of the so-called untouchables. Gandhi called them *harijans,* "the children of God," and begged his fellow Indians to banish untouchability from their hearts and lives. This message must be proclaimed in every part of the world today, including the United States, so that no one will be marginalized. Solidarity in our own society might mean touching the lives of those marginalized by our culture—gays and lesbians, people of color, "illegal aliens," the elderly, people with disabilities, people with AIDS, and others.

Gandhi also developed a practical "constructive program" to rid India and the world of poverty and injustice. He lived with the poor and taught them ways to improve their lives, while always advocating voluntary poverty and simplicity of life. He tried to improve the environment, improve public sanitation, and encourage the personal responsibility of daily work. Gandhi's creed was: Recall the face of the poorest and the most helpless person you have seen and ask yourself if the step you contemplate is going to be of any use to that person. Will he or she be able to gain anything by it?

Today, it is more essential than ever for us to learn the lessons of Gandhi's nonviolent resistance. Perhaps the primary lesson we must relearn from Gandhi is to choose, every day for the rest of our lives, the truth of nonviolence over the lie of nuclear violence and every other form of violence and injustice. Gandhi's path to nonviolence—the way of the cross—is an invitation individually to resist the nuclear arms race, and to allow that resistance to flourish publicly in our lives.

In his autobiographical essay, "Pilgrimage to Nonviolence," Martin Luther King, Jr., tells how he "became deeply fascinated" with the life and teachings of Gandhi:

Gandhi was probably the first person in history to lift the love ethic of Jesus above mere interaction between individuals to a powerful and effective social force on a large scale. For Gandhi love was a potent instrument for social and collective transformation. It was in this Gandhian emphasis on love and nonviolence that I discovered the method for social reform that I had been seeking for so many months. . . . I came to feel that this was the only morally and practically sound method open to oppressed people in their struggle for freedom.[7]

On August 6, 1945, at the beginning of the nuclear age, Gandhi wrote, "Unless now the world adopts nonviolence, it will spell certain suicide for humanity. . . . Nonviolence is the only thing the atom bomb cannot destroy."[8] Shortly after the bombing of Hiroshima and Nagasaki, he reflected that the bomb made clear to the world that war is the mass pursuit of death.

So far as I can see, the atomic bomb has deadened the finest feeling that has sustained humanity for ages. There used to be the so-called laws of war which made it intolerable. Now we know the naked truth. War knows no law except that of might. The atom bomb brought an empty victory to the allied arms, but it resulted for the time being in destroying the soul of Japan. What has happened to the soul of the destroying nation is yet too early to see.[9]

Hours before he was assassinated, Gandhi was asked by an American journalist how he would meet the atomic bomb with nonviolence. While it may seem difficult to confront such violence and destruction, Gandhi had an answer. "I will not go underground. I will not go into shelter. I will come out in the open and let the pilot see I have not a trace of ill-will against him. The pilot will not see our faces from his great height, I know. But the longing in our hearts—that he will not come to harm—would reach up to him and his eyes would be opened."[10]

Theologian Jim Douglass has written that Jesus spoke of the coming of the kingdom of God as "lightning striking in the east and flashing far into the west," and that our choice of lightning east to west today is between nuclear fire and the kingdom of God, despair and annihilation or transformation through nonviolence. "If we look to Jesus and Gandhi, and what they point to," Douglass suggests,

We can hope to choose the lightning fire of nonviolence. . . . The symbols and prophets of the kingdom of Reality are Jesus and Gandhi: Jesus, the kingdom's proclaimer and symbol in the West (but himself a Jew from the Mid-East); Gandhi, the kingdom's symbol in the East (but himself a student of the West in his reading of Thoreau, Tolstoy and Ruskin). Their kingdom of nonviolent truth-force and love-force if realized would be a lightning east to west, the energy equivalent and alternative to a nuclear fire ending the world.[11]

Ultimately, Gandhi's message of nonviolence for Americans today is a call to resist the nuclear arms race. As the struggle for peace continues, we must return to Gandhi's satyagraha campaigns, study his discoveries, and seek to apply them in our own local work to rid the land of weapons and ourselves from the arms race within. "We have to make truth and nonviolence not matters for mere individual practice but for practice by groups and communities and nations. That at any rate is my dream. I shall live and die in trying to realize it."[12]

Nonviolence, the power of the powerless is, Gandhi believed, the power of God, the power of truth and love that goes beyond the physical world into the realm of the spiritual. It can overcome death, as God revealed through the nonviolence of Jesus, his crucifixion, and subsequent resurrection in the resisting community. Gandhi sought this power on a public level as no one else in modern times has done. He offered a way to demonstrate love as a method for social change. The key for Gandhi was to raise to the public level the deep nonviolent love that lay within the individual. "Nonviolence is not a cloistered virtue to be practiced by the individual for his or her peace and final salvation, but it is a rule of conduct for society. . . . I hold it therefore to be wrong to limit the use of nonviolence to cave dwellers (hermits) and for acquiring merit for a favored position in the other world. All virtue ceases to have use if it serves no purpose in every walk of life."[13]

Gandhi's belief in nonviolence was rooted equally in his Hindu tradition and in the nonviolence of Jesus' example and words, especially in the Sermon on the Mount and the cross. Gandhi wrote that

Jesus was the most active resister known perhaps to history. This was nonviolence par excellence. . . . Jesus, a person who was completely innocent, offered himself as a sacrifice for the good of others, including his enemies, and became the ransom of the world. It was a perfect act. . . . Jesus lived and died in vain if He did not teach us to regulate the whole of life by the eternal law of love.[14]

As Ignatius Jesudasan points out in his study *A Gandhian Theology of Liberation*, Gandhi mourned the fact that people who claimed to believe in the message of Jesus, whom they described as the Prince of Peace, put little of that belief into practice. Gandhi wanted "to convince honest doubters that the love that Jesus taught and practiced was not a mere personal virtue, but that it was essentially a social and collective virtue." Gandhi wrote:

I rebel against orthodox Christianity, as I am convinced that it has distorted the message of Jesus. He was an Asiatic whose message was delivered through many media and when it had the backing of the

Roman emperor, it became an imperialist faith as it remains to this day.[15]

Christianity had yet to put into practice the nonviolence Jesus taught and lived, Gandhi maintained. He urged Christians to turn to the cross as the way of liberation for humanity.

Gandhi's goal was the spiritual liberation of humanity, a freedom that would have real political consequences here and now. He wanted the kingdom of God that is within each person to be realized and to be extended throughout humanity so that oppression, injustice, and violence would cease and love and truth would reign. "When the practice of the law (truth and love) becomes universal, God will reign on earth as God does in Heaven. Earth and Heaven are in us. We know the earth, and we are strangers to the heaven within us."[16]

Gandhi's lifelong pursuit of truth and love led him to practice nonviolent resistance in a variety of areas. He and his colleagues resisted the violence and death that lay at the heart of untouchability, sexism, racism, war, colonization, religious division, and the nuclear arms race. His participation in these struggles resulted in his imprisonment, physical abuse, and eventual assassination. But Gandhi had pledged his life to seek justice and peace without the use of violence; he willingly accepted the punishment meted out to him. He had offered to sacrifice his life for peace and justice. He went to jail smiling. He was killed while offering a sign of peace. These acts of resistance done in this spirit of nonviolence epitomized the message of Gandhi:

A *satyagrahi* must always be ready to die with a smile on [her] face, without retaliation and without rancor in [her] heart. Some people have come to have a wrong notion that *satyagraha* means only jail-going, perhaps facing blows, and nothing more. Such *satyagraha* cannot bring independence. To win independence you have to learn the art of dying without killing.[17]

Gandhi's twentieth-century experiments in truth point to the way of the cross, the way of nonviolent love and resistance. His gift is the example of a life committed to nonviolent resistance and seeking God's justice first. He was a faithful Hindu who invites us to explore the depths of love and truth in our own faiths, and to become renewed in the spirit of love and truth. He was quite clear about the breadth of nonviolent activity that must be pursued in the nuclear age, if humanity is to live. "Several lives like mine will have to be given if the terrible violence that has spread all over is to stop and nonviolence reign supreme in its place."[18]

Gandhi's life must be explored today with renewed vigor. We need to study his message, his life, and the scriptures that gave him strength. Then, we must join with others in our own U.S. ashrams, base communities of nonviolent resistance, to begin the work of nonviolent love with a deeper commitment. We must cultivate the spirit of love and truth in our own lives through our own modern-day experiments in love and truth, which may lead us to public acts of loving disobedience to government authority.

One of Gandhi's associates, Asha Devi, was asked by a BBC interviewer, "Don't you think that Gandhi was a bit unrealistic, that he failed to reckon with the limits of our capacities?" Devi responded, "There are no limits to our capacities."[19]

Gandhi discovered that indeed there are no limits to our capacities, that the God of nonviolent love is with us. In the nuclear age, a time of despairing spirits and policies of war, Gandhi recaptured the boundless hope of Jesus who invited his disciples to become perfect as God is perfect. Gandhi sought to become perfect, compassionate, as Jesus suggested. He endeavored to live nonviolence, in his heart and in the public arena, and God was with him. Gandhi offers a contemporary example of struggling for liberation through Jesus' way of nonviolent resistance. Gandhi demonstrated to the world with new vigor that God indeed wants us to know the truth and to be set free. "Where there is God there is truth, and where there is truth, there is God. I love truth only," Gandhi said, "and so God is with me."[20] Gandhi's life of nonviolence and resistance may be the best modern-day example of discipleship to Jesus. If Christians can embrace the Sermon on the Mount as now explained by Gandhi in the spirit of Jesus, perhaps the disarmament of the world will begin and love will reign on earth as love reigns in heaven.

Our God Is Nonviolent

Notes

1. Eknath Easawaran, *Gandhi the Man* (Petaluma, Calif.: Nilgiria Press, 1978), 145.

2. Mohandas Gandhi, *All Men Are Brothers* (New York: Continuum, 1982), 3–4.

3. James Douglass, *The Nonviolent Cross* (New York: Macmillan Co., 1968), 36.

4. Thomas Merton, ed., *Gandhi on Nonviolence* (New York: New Directions, 1965), 44–45.

5. Easawaran, *Gandhi the Man*, 112–16, 152.

6. Ibid., 169.

7. Martin Luther King, Jr., "Pilgrimage to Nonviolence," in James Washington, ed., *A Testament of Hope* (San Francisco: Harper & Row, 1986), 38.

8. Merton, *Gandhi on Nonviolence*, 33.

9. Ibid., 32.

10. James Douglass, *Lightning East to West* (New York: Crossroad, 1984), 42.

11. Ibid., ix, 18.

12. Easawaran, *Gandhi the Man*, 129.

13. Ibid., 155.

14. Merton, *Gandhi on Nonviolence*, 26, 34, 40.

15. Ignatius Jesudasan, *A Gandhian Theology of Liberation* (Maryknoll, N.Y.: Orbis Books, 1984), 114–15.

16. Douglass, *Lightning East to West*, 39.

17. Merton, *Gandhi on Nonviolence*, 49.

18. Ibid., 73.

19. Easawaran, *Gandhi on Nonviolence*, 8.

20. Jesudasan, *Gandhian Theology*, 67.

4

Martin Luther King, Jr.

"OUR GOD IS ABLE"

Martin Luther King, Jr., is the foremost prophet of the God of nonviolence in the United States. Through King's life and the civil rights movement he led, God revealed the power of active love to transform injustice. Thousands of Americans moved out of the slavery of segregation and oppression toward greater freedom and faith in God. This extraordinary example shook the nation and provided us with a modern-day way of living the nonviolence of the gospel within our own culture.

Through his active practice of nonviolence, King called for the conversion of all people to the truth of nonviolence. He called for the complete expression of nonviolence: liberation into the beloved community. When all people are nonviolent, King dreamed, then all people will be free.

King's civil rights and peace activism provided the base for his theology of liberation centered in nonviolent resistance. He sought to stand in solidarity with the poor, the oppressed, and the victims of violence, and to seek their liberation because he saw God doing just that. King's vision was the vision of God's kingdom where all are reconciled, where all love one another and live in peace and justice.

This vision, rooted in faith and praxis, motivated King to march almost daily for the cause of justice. But it is a vision that still waits for our understanding and implementation. Though King is recognized with a national holiday and schools and streets bear his name, his message has been diluted. He has been made acceptable, and hence less radical. King's life message still waits to be heard and put into practice.

Time and time again, like a prophet of old, King laid out his message of peace:

There is no easy way to create a world where men and women can live together, where each has their own job and house and where all children receive as much education as their minds can absorb. But if such a world is created in our lifetime, it will be done in the United States by black and white people of good will. It will be accomplished by persons who have the courage to put an end to suffering by willingly suffering themselves rather than inflict suffering upon others. It will be done by rejecting the racism, materialism and violence that has characterized Western civilization and especially by working toward a world of brotherhood and sisterhood, cooperation and peace.[1]

King believed in God and God's presence in all nonviolent struggles for justice and peace. "We must be reminded anew that God is at work in [God's] universe. God is not outside the world looking on with a sort of cold indifference. Here on all the roads of life, God is striving in our striving. Like an ever-loving Father, God is working through history for the salvation of [God's] children. As we struggle to defeat the forces of evil, the God of the universe struggles with us."[2]

For King, God is moral, human life has meaning, and history has a goal—the creation of the beloved community. King believed that all of life is interrelated and that all persons are caught "in an inescapable network of mutuality, tied in a single garment of destiny. Whatever affects one directly, affects all indirectly." Segregation destroyed community and made brotherhood and sisterhood impossible.

King's God is both good and powerful, capable of overcoming all evil, a belief that he maintained and that grew stronger during his campaigns for peace and justice.

A God devoid of power is ultimately incapable of actualizing the good. But if God is truly God and warrants humanity's ultimate devotion, God must have not only an infinite concern for the good but an infinite power to actualize the good.[3]

This faith in a just and an active God sustained King through his life, and became the source of King's strength, as he recalled:

The agonizing moments through which I have passed during the last few years have also drawn me closer to God. More than ever before I am convinced of the reality of a personal God. True, I have always believed in the personality of God. But in the past the idea of a personal God was little more than a metaphysical category that I found theologically and philosophically satisfying. Now it is a living reality that has been validated in the experiences of everyday life. God has been profoundly real to me in recent years. In the midst of lonely days and dreary nights I have heard an inner voice saying, "Lo, I will be with you." When the chains of fear and the manacles of frustration have all but stymied my efforts, I have felt the power of God transforming the fatigue of despair into the buoyancy of hope. I am convinced that the universe is under the control of a loving purpose, and that in the struggle for righteousness humanity has cosmic companionship. Behind the harsh appearances of the world there is a benign power. . . . In the truest sense of the word, God is a living God. In God there is feeling and will, responsive to the deepest yearnings of the human heart. This God both evokes and answers prayer.[4]

Through this deep faith, King came to understand the gospel call to nonviolence. His personal odyssey with nonviolence grew from a tactic of resistance to a way of life. Gandhi's example influenced him deeply. "Christ furnished the spirit and motivation while Gandhi furnished the method," King wrote.

King spent his public life pleading the cause of gospel nonviolence and conversion from hate to *agape.* "Nonviolence," King explained, "is the answer to the crucial political and moral question of our time—the need for humanity to overcome oppression and violence without resorting to violence and oppression."[5] He sought to reconcile blacks and whites together as the children of God they already were. On January 30, 1956, his home was bombed, and when hundreds of angry people gathered at the site, many of them armed and ready to shoot it out with the police, King insisted on nonviolent love:

We cannot solve this problem through retaliatory violence. . . . We must love our white brothers no matter what they do to us. We must make them know that we love them. Jesus still cries out in words that echo across the centuries: "Love your enemies; bless them that curse you; pray for them that despitefully use you." This is what we must live by. We must meet hate with love.[6]

King's constant appeal to Jesus' message of love was rooted in his understanding of God as the God of love and religion as the practice of the will of God: Love your enemies; love one another.

One cannot remove an evil habit by mere resolution nor by simply calling on God to do the job, but only as one surrenders oneself and becomes an instrument of God. We shall be delivered from the accumulated weight of evil only when we permit the energy of God to come into our souls. Any religion that professes to be concerned with the souls of men and women and is not concerned with the slums that damn them and the social conditions that cripple them is a dry-as-dust religion. Religion deals with both heaven and earth, time and eternity, seeking not only to integrate men and women with God but men and women with men and women.[7]

"The command to love one's enemy is an absolute necessity for our survival," King said often. "Love even for enemies is the key to the solution of the problem of our world. Jesus is not an impractical idealist; he is the practical realist."[8]

King's pilgrimage of nonviolence took him from the Montgomery boycott through a campaign in "the most racist city in the South," Birmingham, Alabama, to a massive, historic march from Selma to Montgomery, Alabama, and eventually to call for massive civil disobedience on a national scale and the application of nonviolence in the international arena. King's efforts became even bolder once he moved to Chicago to continue the work for justice and began to share the life of the poor and oppressed. His solidarity with the poor of the world and his commitment to a love that encompasses one's enemies led to his early death. He offered his life to the struggle, the international nonviolent revolution:

I choose to identify with the underprivileged. I choose to identify with the poor. I choose to give my life to the hungry. I choose to give my life for those who have been left out of the sunlight of opportunity. I choose to live for and with those who find themselves seeing life as a long and desolate corridor with no exit sign. This is the way I'm going. If it means suffering a little bit, I'm going that way. If it means sacrificing, I'm going that way. If it means dying for them, I'm going that way, because I heard a voice saying, "Do something for others."[9]

King's stand against the Vietnam war—which was rooted completely in nonviolence—infuriated the administration and many civil rights supporters, but he was determined to remain consistently nonviolent, faithful to the gospel. "It is worthless to talk about integrating if there is no world to integrate in," he would say. As early as 1958, he had stated that "the goal of all nations must be the total abandonment of the concept of war and a firm commitment to disarmament." Either war must be eliminated or humankind would be eliminated, King asserted. He called for nonviolence in international relations and spoke out against nuclear preparations:

I now believe that the potential destructiveness of modern weapons totally rules out the possibility of war ever again achieving a negative good. If we assume that humankind has a right to survive, then we must find an alternative to war and destruction. In our day of space vehicles and guided ballistic missiles, the choice is either nonviolence or nonexistence. . . . I am convinced that the church cannot be silent while humankind faces the threat of nuclear annihilation. If the church is true to her mission, she must call for an end to the arms race.[10]

King's speech upon receiving the Nobel Peace Prize on December 10, 1964, in Oslo, Norway, was an affirmation of the power of nonviolence, and the hope of a more just world:

I have the audacity to believe that peoples everywhere can have three meals a day for their bodies, education and culture for their minds, and dignity, equality and freedom for their spirits. I believe that what self-centered men and women have torn down, other-centered men and women can build up. I still believe that one day humankind will bow before the altars of God and be crowned triumphant over war and bloodshed, and nonviolent redemptive goodwill will proclaim the rule of the land.[11]

King entered into the political and economic struggle for freedom, not only for blacks but for poor whites and all oppressed peoples. King was assassinated while fighting for the rights of striking garbage workers in Memphis and planning the Poor People's March in Washington, D.C. In the "Poor People's Campaign," King sought to bring together all the poor and oppressed in the nation to demand liberation and justice. "America has not met its obligations and its responsibilities to the poor," Dr. King said throughout his travels in preparation for the campaign. His work for justice and peace, rooted in steadfast active nonviolence, was prophetic and revolutionary, a threat to the normal, violent way of life.

William Watley has identified six major principles that King developed into a nonviolent ethic:

1. Nonviolence is the way of the strong, not a method of the cowardly
2. The goals of nonviolent resistance are always redemption, reconciliation, and winning the enemy's friendship and understanding, not the humiliation or defeat of the opponent
3. The opponent is a symbol of a greater evil; nonviolence is directed against the forces of evil rather than against the person who committed the evil, with the understanding that the evildoers are victims of evil as much as are the individuals and communities that the evildoers oppressed
4. Suffering that is accepted without retaliation is redemptive
5. Love—*agape*—is the center of nonviolence, so violence and hatred must be both resisted and avoided
6. The universe is on the side of justice

Watley concludes that the most important and essential lesson Christians can learn from King is that "oppression and evil must be resisted."[12]

King's brilliant public statement condemning the war in Vietnam, delivered in April 1967, not only pointed out his commitment to nonviolence, the connections with the war in Vietnam and the war on the poor at home, and the hypocrisy of sending blacks to fight for freedom thousands of miles away when they were not free in the United States, but also pointed out that the Vietnam war was symptomatic of a deeper malady of the American spirit:

Clergy and Laity-Concerned Committees for the next generation . . . will be concerned about Guatemala and Peru. They will be concerned about Thailand and Cambodia. They will be concerned about Mozambique and South Africa. We will be marching for these and a dozen other names and attending rallies without end unless there is a significant and profound change in American life and policy. Such thoughts take us beyond Vietnam, but not beyond our calling as sons and daughters of the living God. . . .
I am convinced that if we are to get on the right side of the world revolution, we as a nation must undergo a radical revolution of values. We must rapidly begin the shift from a "thing-oriented" society to a "person-oriented" society. . . . We still have a choice today: nonviolent coexistence or violent co-annihilation.[13]

King's dream found its roots in his particular American experience and in his church. He challenged the centuries-old assumption that violence is more powerful, and he argued through his actions and speeches that nonviolence is more powerful. "Nonviolence is a powerful and just weapon. It is a weapon unique in history, which cuts without wounding and ennobles the one who wields it. It is a sword that heals. Both a practical and moral answer to the oppressed people's cry for justice, nonviolent direct action proved that it could win victories without losing wars."[14]

King's total commitment is reflected in a remark he made in 1967 when an old school friend stopped by King's home in Atlanta for a visit. The friend had been disturbed by King's outspoken stance against the war in Vietnam. King explained to him:

You've never really given this organization full credit for what it really stands for. . . . It's a nonviolent organization, and when I say nonviolent

I mean nonviolent all the way. . . . Never could I advocate nonviolence in this country and not advocate nonviolence for the whole world. . . . That's my philosophy. I don't believe in the death and killing on any side, no matter who's heading it up—whether it be America or any other country, or whether it be blacks. . . . Nonviolence is my stand, and I'll die for that stand.[15]

In his tireless pursuit of justice and peace, King pointed to God who is nonviolent love, and then he acted out the will of his nonviolent God. Love is God and we are called to live lives of nonviolent love, King taught all who would listen. In one of his earliest sermons, King declared, "I still believe that love is the most durable power in the world. . . . I think I have discovered the highest good. It is love. This principle stands at the center of the cosmos. As John says, 'God is love.' The one who loves is a participant in the being of God."[16]

Through the nonviolent love of disciples, God is redeeming humanity and liberating it from all division. Our God is able, King preached, to liberate the world of all violence, oppression, and war. God is able to sustain the universe, to conquer the evils of history, and to give us interior resources to confront the injustices of the world. "When our days become dreary with low-hovering clouds and our nights become darker than a thousand midnights, let us remember that there is a great benign Power in the universe whose name is God, and God is able to make a way out of no way, and transform dark yesterdays into bright tomorrows. This is our hope for becoming better men and women. This is our mandate for seeking to make a better world."[17]

King's contribution to Americans goes beyond his civil rights and peace work to the very simple witness of his deep faith in a nonviolent God who calls us to be nonviolent. He became one of the heroes of nonviolent resistance in history. He demonstrated how faith and love could be put into action and positively affect the most pressing social and political concerns of the day. He brought the needs of the poor and oppressed and the horrors of war to the attention of the nation. He showed that everyone can do something to create a better world and to make the dream of a beloved community a reality. Unfortunately, while society honors King the hero, it turns a deaf ear to his message and dream. Our challenge is to make that dream live.

Martin Luther King, Jr.

Notes

1. Martin Luther King, Jr., "Nonviolence: The Only Road to Freedom," in James M. Washington, ed., *A Testament of Hope: The Essential Writings of Martin Luther King, Jr.* (San Francisco: Harper & Row, 1986), 61.

2. William D. Watley, *Roots of Resistance: The Nonviolent Ethic of Martin Luther King, Jr.* (Valley Forge, Pa.: Judson Press, 1985), 24–25.

3. Ibid., 41.

4. Ibid., 44.

5. King, "Nobel Prize Acceptance Speech," in Washington, ed., *Testament of Hope*, 224.

6. William Robert Miller, *Nonviolence* (New York: Schocken Books, 1964), 63–64.

7. Coretta Scott King, ed., *The Words of Martin Luther King, Jr.* (New York: Newmarket Press, 1983), 66.

8. Martin Luther King, Jr., *Strength to Love* (Philadelphia: Fortress Press, 1981), 47.

9. Vincent Harding, "We Must Keep Going: Martin Luther King, Jr. and the Future of America," *Fellowship* (Jan./Feb. 1987): 7.

10. Martin Luther King, Jr., *Strength to Love*, 152–53.

11. King, "Nobel Prize Acceptance Speech," in Washington, ed., *Testament of Hope*, 224–25.

12. Watley, *Roots of Resistance*, 111–28.

13. King, "A Time to Break Silence," in Washington, ed., *Testament of Hope*, 240.

14. Harding, "We Must Keep Going," 16.

15. David Garrow, *Bearing the Cross: Martin Luther King, Jr. and the Southern Christian Leadership Conference* (New York: William Morrow, 1986), 572–73.

16. King, "Facing the Challenge of a New Age," in Washington, ed., *Testament of Hope*, 137.

17. King, "Our God Is Able," in Washington, ed., *Testament of Hope*, 509.

5

Dorothy Day

"THE ONLY SOLUTION IS LOVE"

When Dorothy Day died in 1980 at the age of eighty-three, she left behind the example of a life of integrity. With Peter Maurin, she founded the Catholic Worker movement, which included communities that offer hospitality to the urban poor, work on farms, a public stand for peace and against war, and a newspaper, *The Catholic Worker*. Day spent her life offering food, shelter, hospitality, and words of hope to millions of people. While living a life of poverty amidst the poor, she challenged the violence and wars of society. Her steadfast commitment to gospel nonviolence was accompanied by her active and equally strong resistance to war and injustice. She lived the life of a saint, but was considered too radical for the Catholic church she loved. Now, after her death, while she is praised and honored, her example is followed by only a handful of the faithful. We see now that her life paved a way of resistance and liberation for the poor and all else who would listen. She put into practice the liberating word of nonviolence and changed the Catholic church in the United States in the process. She invited Christians to take their faith seriously.

The authenticity of Day's life was perhaps her greatest gift to us. She practiced what she preached, did what she urged others to do, gave up

all her possessions as she advised others, and prayed every day as she recommended all others do. She possessed a strong vision of the church and what it meant to be a Christian, and she struggled to be true to that vision. Throughout her long life, she remained faithful to the vision of the gospel. During the depression, World War II, the Korean war, the civil rights movement, the Vietnam war, and the nuclear arms buildup, she clung to the truth of nonviolence, voluntary poverty, the works of mercy, community, and faith. She abandoned herself to Divine Providence, resisted the warfare state, served its victims, and sought out the way of the cross at every turn. "As you come to know the seriousness of our situation—the war, the racism, the poverty in the world—you come to realize it is not going to be changed by words or demonstrations," Day once said. "It's a question of risking your life. It's a question of living your life in drastically different ways."[1] Day risked her life for the poor and for peace. She was not recognized by presidents or popes, yet her witness stands with that of Francis of Assisi and Gandhi.

Day's concern was poverty; her emphasis was always on serving the poor. "Poverty is my vocation, to live as simply and as poorly as I can, and never to cease talking and writing of poverty and destitution," she wrote.[2] Quoting Eugene Debs, she claimed, "While there are poor, I am one of them. While men and women are in prison, I am not free." She embraced voluntary poverty for herself, as strictly as possible, but while finding her fulfillment as a Christian in this freely chosen poverty, she refused to accept the destitution suffered by and inflicted on others. "We were ready to 'endure wrongs patiently' for ourselves . . . but we were not going to be meek for others, enduring their wrongs patiently." The poor were "nearest to God . . . chosen by Christ for his compassion," she discovered. She repeated Eric Gill's observation, that "Christ came to make the rich poor and the poor holy."[3]

Yes, the poor are always going to be with us—our Lord told us that—and there will always be a need for our sharing, for stripping ourselves to help others. It will always be a lifetime job. But I am sure that God did not intend that there be so many poor. The class structure is of *our* making and *our* consent, not God's, and we must do what we can to change it. So we are urging revolutionary change.[4]

73

Day sought to free others from the misery of involuntary poverty, which only inflamed the appetite for worldly things. She wanted to lead people to the voluntary poverty she had chosen, which freed her from the appetite for worldly possessions, riches, honors, and pride. "I condemn poverty and I advocate it," she once wrote. This life of poverty became one complete act of resistance. "Anything you do not need belongs to the poor," she repeated often.

Once we begin not to worry about what kind of house we are living in, what kind of clothes we are wearing, once we give up the stupid recreation of the world, we have time which is priceless—to remember that we are all our brothers' and sisters' keepers and that we must not only care for their needs as far as we are immediately able, but we must try to build a better world.[5]

Day understood love as the emptying of oneself as Christ did, as the acceptance of poverty. Such love resisted the consumeristic trends of society.

Love of brother and sister means voluntary poverty, stripping one's self, putting off the old person, denying one's self, etc. It also means non-participation in those comforts and luxuries which have been manufactured by the exploitation of others. While our brothers and sisters suffer, we must be compassionate with them, suffer with them. While our brothers and sisters suffer from lack of necessities, we will refuse to enjoy comforts.[6]

By living poorly with the poor, Day presented a life style of radical holiness that stood in complete contrast to the life style admired by her own country, the world's wealthiest and most militaristic nation. Her pacifism was a necessary corollary to her voluntary poverty, a necessary part of the gospel of Jesus. She knew that greed was behind war: people fight to defend their possessions. Thus her voluntary poverty was a stand against war. She and her Catholic Worker colleagues were adamant in their gospel evangelization for peace and justice. She understood the connection between the works of peace and justice in nonviolent resistance, and the works of mercy and charity performed in houses of hospitality. This was her genius, and her gift to us.

One of her favorite parables came from Ignazio Silone's novel, *Bread and Wine*. The story provided an image that propelled her to speak out against violence:

In that book, [there is a] man [who] is a communist. The communists in Italy are always religious; he's disguised as a priest and he's hiding up in the mountains. When Mussolini declares war on Ethiopia, he runs out and chalks up "No!" on all the buildings. A girl, the loose woman of the town, is trying to take care of him. She says, "What did you do a foolish thing like that for?" He replies, "One person shouting 'No' is enough to break the unanimity." I thought that was the most beautiful thing to say.[7]

Day's life became one consistent No! against violence, injustice, and war. Her civil disobedience further enacted the gospel teachings she sought to live. As mentioned in chapter 1, in the late 1950s she was repeatedly arrested for refusing to take shelter during compulsory civil defense drills. Eventually the drills were stopped, thanks in part to her witness. In 1972, at the age of seventy-five, she was arrested in California for protesting with Cesar Chavez on behalf of exploited farm workers. On August 6, 1976, the anniversary of the bombing of Hiroshima, Day made her last speaking appearance before a large audience at the Catholic Eucharist Conference in Philadelphia. She asked why the church conference had not set aside the day for a time of penance and sorrow and spoke out against further preparations for nuclear war.

Not everyone is called to become a Catholic Worker, she agreed, but all are called to work for justice and peace, "to do what we can, and the whole field of all the works of mercy is open to us."[8] She understood well the connection between doing the works of mercy and at the same time not doing the works of war. To seek peace, she asked Christians to choose voluntary poverty: "All our talks about peace and the weapons of the spirit are meaningless unless we try in every way to embrace voluntary poverty and not work in any position, any job, that contributes to war, not to take any job whose pay comes from the fear of war, or the atomic bomb." Later she explained, "It is voluntary poverty which needs to be preached to the comfortable congregations so that people will not be afraid of losing their jobs if they speak out on these issues."⁹ Voluntary poverty, she said, is the only way we have of showing our love.

Within the church, Day was a prophet for peace, urging clerics and lay people to accept pacifism and to serve the poor. Addressing the U.S. bishops she said, "Get rid of all your worldly advisors. This whole business of investing: it's usury. It's condemned in the catechism, in the same class as the seven deadly sins, as sodomy. Money doesn't breed money. Don't invest money, except in the poor—there you might expect a return."¹⁰

As the spiritual leader of the Catholic Worker movement, Day inspired a wide variety of Christians to a greater commitment to Jesus' way of nonviolent suffering love and personal responsibility for the needy. In the Houses of Hospitality, the farms for communal retreat, reflection, study sessions, talks, acts of nonviolent civil disobedience, worship, and writing, the Catholic Worker movement has grown to lead the Christian communities in the United States to a deeper commitment to the gospel. Ultimately, what Day urged was that everyone strive for sanctity and take the gospel seriously. "Becoming a saint is the revolution," she said frequently. She insisted that the conversion of society began with the interior conversion of the person to God, to the gospel life style of love, prayer, peace, and justice. Day demonstrated that when Christians fulfill their callings and become saints, they live lives of nonviolent resistance.

Day's life of nonviolent action and service was founded in prayer and faith. Without a grounding in prayer, she recognized, people can become very discouraged. Near the end of her life, she read the Psalms, the Gospels and the New Testament every day between six and eight in the morning. Faithful prayer to God sustained her through the many trying circumstances of prison, sickness, mounting bills, criticism, pressures, and the needs of the homeless, hungry, oppressed people who came to her and the Catholic Worker community for help. Her commitment to nonviolence followed the little way of St. Therese of Lisieux in its simple, childlike, and even Buddhist trust.

When I lie in jail, thinking of war and peace and the problems of human freedom and the apathy of great masses of people who believe that nothing can be done, I am all the more confirmed in my faith in the little way of St. Therese of Lisieux. We do the minute things that come to hand, we pray our prayers, and beg also for an increase of faith—and God will do the rest.[11]

Much of Day's work on behalf of the gospel took the form of writing. She was a journalist for peace, a modern-day evangelist. She wrote books, essays, and thousands of newspaper columns, all reflecting on the theology she lived day to day.[12] In this way, she shared her insights and taught the theology of peace and resistance which she learned from experience.

The essence of Day's life centered on two truths: (1) Jesus Christ is present in the distressing disguise of the poor and the oppressed; and (2) Jesus Christ is also present in the distressing disguise of our enemies. We are called to love Christ both in the poor and in our enemies, she realized. To fail to love these despised human beings is to fail to love Christ. She often turned to Matthew 25 and the Sermon on the Mount for guidance: "I was hungry and you gave me food; I was thirsty and you gave me drink. I was a stranger and you welcomed me, naked and you clothed me. I was ill and you comforted me, in prison and you came to visit me. . . . As often as you did this for one of the least of these, you did it for me." "Love your enemies, pray for your persecutors. This will prove that you are sons and daughters of your God, for God's sun rises on the bad and the good. God rains on the just and unjust." Her prayer was simple: "Dear God, please enlarge our hearts to love each other, to love our neighbor, to love our enemy as well as our friend."[13]

Radical love—the love of Christ for others—consumed Day and formed the mission of her life. "All my prayer, my own suffering, my reading, my study, would lead me to this conclusion. This is a great and holy force and must be used as the spiritual weapon. Love against hate. Suffering against violence. What is two thousand years in the history of the world? We have scarcely begun to love. We have scarcely begun to know Christ, to see him in others around us . . ."[14] These reflections from one of her retreats summed up her life goal: the work of nonviolent love.

She concluded her famous autobiography, *The Long Loneliness*, on this theme of love:

The most significant thing about the Catholic Worker is poverty, some say. The most significant thing is community, others say. We are not alone any more. But the final word is love. At times it has been, in the words of Father Zossima, a harsh and dreadful thing, and our very faith in love has been tried through fire. We cannot love God unless we love each other, and to love we must know each other. We know God in the breaking of bread and we know each other in the breaking of bread, and we are not alone any more. Heaven is a banquet, too, even with a crust, where there is companionship. We have all known the long loneliness, and we have learned that the only true solution is love, and love comes with community. It all happened while we sat there talking, and it is still going on.[15]

Day focused her entire spirit on the liberation of the poor through gospel nonviolence. Her constant vision was of the peaceable kingdom of Jesus, where the last are given first place. In her lifework of liberation through nonviolent love, she incarnated a preferential option for the poor and a preferential option for peace and justice. She attempted to lay down her life for those in need within the context of the United States, in the immediate world of New York City's Lower East Side. She tried to love humanity and to love God. Her resistance to the violence and injustices of society were countered by her irrepressible hope in God. This hope gave her the strength to live a long life of service and nonviolence and resistance. She was a faithful servant pointing to a way of liberation through a radically different life style. She proved that we in the United States can be liberated from despair, greed, and violence by living out that liberation.

As we struggle to risk our lives for the needy and for peace and to live the gospel, it is important to remember Day's model of a committed, faithful life. She did not gain world attention or media coverage. She did what she could, quietly, peacefully, patiently, relying solely on the force of truth, doing the good because it was right to do it. Because of this fidelity, history will know her as one of the greatest examples of nonviolent love in action. Through her words and actions, she invites us to take up that work of nonviolence where she left off—and to be faithful to the will of our God. May her example give us strength.

Notes

1. Arthur Laffin and Anne Montgomery, *Swords into Plowshares* (San Francisco: Harper & Row, 1985), 20.

2. David J. O'Brien, "The Pilgrimage of Dorothy Day," *Commonweal* (December 19, 1980): 714.

3. Dale Vree, "A Radical Holiness," *Commonweal* (May 6, 1983): 266–69.

4. Robert Ellsberg, ed., *By Little and By Little: The Selected Writings of Dorothy Day* (New York: Alfred A. Knopf, 1983), 111.

5. Margaret Quigley and Michael Garvey, eds., *The Dorothy Day Book* (Springfield, Ill.: Templegate Pub., 1982).

6. Dorothy Day, *Meditations,* selected by Stanley Vishnewski, 252.

7. Jim Wallis and Wes Michaelson, "Interview with Dorothy Day: Exalting Those of Low Degree," A *Sojourners* Reprint, from *Sojourners* (December, 1976).

8. O'Brien, "Pilgrimage of Dorothy Day," 713.

9. Day, *Meditations,* 46–47, 57.

10. Wallis and Michaelson, "Interview with Dorothy Day."

11. Ellsberg, *By Little and By Little,* 285.

12. For further information, see Robert Ellsberg's "Introduction," in *By Little and By Little.*

13. Patrick Jordan, "Dorothy Day: Still a Radical," *Commonweal* (November 29, 1985): 667.

14. William Miller, "Dorothy Day, 1897–1980: 'All Was Grace,' " *America* (December 13, 1980): 385.

15. Dorothy Day, *The Long Loneliness* (San Francisco: Harper & Row, 1981), 285–86.

6

Ita Ford, Maura Clarke, Dorothy Kazel, Jean Donovan

"CHRIST INVITES US NOT TO FEAR PERSECUTION"

Let us kill the dreamer and see what becomes of the dream.

—Gen. 37:20

Just as Joseph faced death threats in the book of Genesis, so have Jesus and all the prophets of nonviolence before and after him, from St. Paul to Martin Luther King, Jr. Throughout Jesus' public life, there were people who wanted to kill him. What was Jesus' dream and why was it such a scandalous threat? The dream of Jesus is something quite specific: "To bring good news to the poor; to proclaim liberty to captives and recovery of sight to the blind; to let the oppressed go free; to proclaim a year acceptable to God" (Luke 4:14–30). Jesus dreamed that we all might be as one in the love and peace of God (John 17:11, 20–21). He dreamed of a kingdom of nonviolence. He was killed for proclaiming this dream of justice and peace, and for living it out, for bringing it into being by resisting everything that went against his dream, but he was irrepressible. He lives! And his dream lives, in the lives and words of his followers, in Christian communities around the world.

To be a Christian, or a churchworker, to be a dreamer in El Salvador, I have learned, is like being a Jew in Nazi Germany. Government death squads hunt people down, especially church workers, and kill them. When I lived and worked in 1985 in a camp for displaced people in El Salvador, I saw thousands of people whose families had been killed, who were homeless, who were persecuted; the daily bombing campaigns sponsored by the U.S. government; military forces everywhere. When I returned to El Salvador in 1988, I saw the repressive U.S.-backed military forces intimidate and harass hundreds of returning refugees. But in the midst of their terrible suffering, the Salvadoran refugees were alive with faith and filled with joy and hope. They had definitely heard good news; Jesus' dream had touched them.

Four great dreamers who took up Jesus' dream of a kingdom of nonviolence and love went about their work quietly in the villages of war-torn El Salvador until they were brutally murdered by the ruling authorities. They were four churchwomen from the United States, dedicated to the poor and the victims of violence and poverty, who served the needy as best they could. As the violence of U.S.-backed military forces increased, leaving dead bodies literally along every Salvadoran roadside, they began to pick up and bury the dead, a work of mercy and justice that was illegal. These four women, Ita Ford, Maura Clarke, Dorothy Kazel, and Jean Donovan, were martyred on December 2, 1980, as they drove home from El Salvador's main airport. They had each come to El Salvador to pursue the dream of Jesus in a land of violence and death. Fifteen miles from the airport, in a deserted field, stands a stone cross marking the calvary where the four were killed. A small plaque reads: "Ita, Maura, Dorothy, and Jean gave their lives on December 2, 1980. Receive them Lord into your kingdom."

What can we learn from these dreamers, these martyrs, these witnesses, these born-again Christians? What happened in their lives? How did they become dreamers, like the Master Dreamer, in a world where it is illegal to dream and where dreamers get killed? Their stories give us a clue and point to a way of liberation: nonviolent solidarity with the poor is a way of resistance and peacemaking.

Ita Ford grew up in Brooklyn, New York, and joined the Maryknoll sisters, a Roman Catholic religious order, in 1961.[1] Because of ill health, she left her community three years later and became a teacher in New York City. Her health improved, and she became active in the civil rights and antiwar movements. In 1970, Ford rejoined Maryknoll and eventually was sent to work and live with the poor of Chile, where she remained throughout the 1970s. The inspiring message of Archbishop Oscar Romero drew her to El Salvador, where she went in the spring of 1980. She arrived shortly after he was assassinated and immediately set to work with the victims of war.

Maura Clarke also grew up in Brooklyn and decided at an early age to become a Maryknoll sister.[2] She spent several years teaching poor children in the Bronx, and then moved to Nicaragua, where she lived and worked under the regime of Anastasio Somoza for seventeen years. Clarke gave herself over entirely to the needs of the poor in a lively village outside Managua. When word came of the crisis in El Salvador in mid-1980, she left her beloved Nicaragua to start a new work—a life of serving the Salvadoran people.

Dorothy Kazel grew up in Cleveland, Ohio, and at age twenty she became engaged to be married.[3] She loved life and lived it to the full. She taught in a parochial school, but just before her wedding, while on retreat, Kazel decided that God wanted her to become a sister in order to serve the poor. So she became an Ursuline sister and eventually joined the Cleveland diocese's mission in El Salvador.

Jean Donovan was a fun-loving, enthusiastic person who was raised in an upper-middle class family from Westport, Connecticut.[4] Her family always voted Republican. Eventually, Donovan became an accountant in Cleveland, Ohio. She was a successful businesswoman who had a lot of money and wanted more. She owned a sports car and a motorcycle, and she enjoyed going out for an evening to argue politics with friends.

But something happened; she began to feel uncomfortable with her life. As she confided to her friend, Father Michael Crowley, a priest in Ireland, her conscience bothered her. She felt an urge to serve the poor. She started to work with young people in the diocese and then volunteered to go to El Salvador to work with the poor. She became a lay missioner, studied at Maryknoll, and at age twenty-seven arrived in El Salvador, in August of 1979.

Missionaries to El Salvador find rampant poverty, brutal civil war, hunger, illiteracy, death squads, corrupt government officials, and lethal weapons donated by the United States. Church workers and community organizers are regularly tortured and killed. The abnormal is normal in El Salvador. Since 1980, over seventy thousand people have been killed there and the United States government has spent $1.7 million a day on military aid to support the violence.[5] When Donovan arrived in 1979, she quickly fell in love with the poor and discovered that they were ministering to her; they became her teachers. Her work primarily involved parish activities—balancing the books and working with youth groups—but in time she became an advocate for the refugees and victims of violence. Like the other three churchwomen, Donovan identified dead bodies and buried them every day. Soon notes were pinned to the bodies saying, "If you bury this body, the same will happen to you." In the summer of 1980, two of Donovan's closest friends, two young Salvadoran men, were brutally murdered across the street from the parish where Donovan and Kazel lived. The horror and pressures of El Salvador led Donovan's friends to urge her to return home. She did return to the United States for a visit, where family and friends asked her not to go back. Her brother and her fiance pleaded with her not to return. Jean knew full well that her life was in serious danger, that the death squads were actively watching people she knew, and that she and the sisters and their friends might be next. During a brief visit she made to Ireland, Father Michael Crowley begged her not to return, telling her, "You will be kidnapped, tortured, and killed. Don't go back."

Apparently, while at Maryknoll, Donovan went into the chapel to spend the afternoon in prayer. Hours later, at deep peace, she decided to return. As one sister told her mother, "Jean was an entirely different woman. She was ready to go back." Her mother says that Donovan "had somehow reconciled herself to what was happening and what she was to do, and she had made her peace with whatever frightening thoughts she had." Donovan returned to El Salvador fully aware of what was going to happen. "Several times I have decided to leave," she wrote to a friend. "I almost could except for the children, the poor bruised victims of adult lunacy. Who would care for them? Whose heart would be so staunch as to favor the reasonable thing in a sea of their tears and loneliness? Not mine, dear friend, not mine."[6]

Meanwhile, Ford and Clarke continued their work in the tense region of Chalatenango, living with few possessions in a simple parish school building. Their church was surrounded by armed soldiers. Ford and Clarke frequently went to the commander's office to plead for the lives of people who had "disappeared."

Wherever the churchwomen went in El Salvador, they discovered that the martyrdom of Archbishop Romero had left a profound impact in the lives of the people. In life, Romero had been the voice of the poor, their advocate and defender. Kazel and Donovan had known Romero and had held an all-night vigil beside his coffin on the evening before his funeral. Donovan had regularly baked chocolate-chip cookies for him.

In death, Romero immediately became an icon for the people, and the focal point for their hopes and prayers to God. His words inspired the missionaries to continue their active ministry to the people, even with the forces of death surrounding them. Romero died as he lived, preaching the radical gospel of nonviolent resistance. Paraphrasing the words of Christ in this example, Romero's message gave the missionaries the strength to risk the consequences of their work:

Those who, in the biblical phrase, would save their lives—that is, those who don't want commitments, who don't want to get into problems, who want to stay outside whatever demands our involvement—they will lose their lives. What a terrible thing to have lived well off, with no suffering, not getting into problems, quite tranquil, quite settled, with good connections—politically, socially, economically—lacking nothing, having everything. To what good? They will lose their lives. But those who for love of me uproot themselves and accompany the people and go with the poor in their suffering and become incarnate and feel as their own the pain and the abuse of the poor—they will secure their lives, because God will reward them. To each one of us, Christ is saying: "If you want your life and mission to be fruitful like mine, do like me." Be converted into a seed that lets itself be buried. Let yourself be killed. Do not be afraid. Those who shun suffering will remain alone and no one is more alone than the selfish. But if you give your life out of love for others, as I give mine for all, you will reap a great harvest. You will have the deepest satisfactions. Therefore, do not fear death or threats. The Lord goes with you.[7]

On November 27, 1980, Ford and Clarke went to Managua, Nicaragua, to attend a Maryknoll conference. It was a reunion of friends and a time for deep faith sharing. On the final evening, Ford spoke of her commitment to the poor, her life with them in a land of death squads, and the threat that she and Clarke felt to their own lives. She shared a quote from Romero with her Maryknoll sisters:

Christ invites us not to fear persecution. Believe me, sisters and brothers, anyone committed to the poor must risk the same fate as the poor. And in El Salvador, we know the fate of the poor: to disappear, to be tortured, to be jailed, and to be found dead.[8]

On Monday, December 2, 1980, Donovan and Kazel drove to the airport to meet Ford and Clarke when they arrived on the flight from Managua. The four women were last seen alive driving out of the airport. Two days later, their bodies were discovered in a makeshift grave about fifteen miles away. They had been raped and shot at close range.

What can we learn from their lives?

They were ordinary women doing ordinary work—serving those in need. But because they chose to do that work under such awful circumstances, they stand out as heroes.

The four heard God's call to make peace and justice with the poor and they accepted that challenge. God invited them to live out Jesus' message of active love in the world; they heard and obeyed, and they remained faithful. They heeded that call and continued their work even when they knew that their lives were at stake. They reveal that discipleship to Christ is a continuing commitment of suffering love, not just a one-time conversion, and that it requires a willingness to lay down our lives for the poor and with the poor, for the dream of justice and peace, a world without war. They demonstrated for us how to act in the face of the persecution and death threats that are a certainty for the disciple: Stand firmly in faith and continue to witness to the gospel. Jesus says to us, as he said to them: "Let go of everything, your goals, your ambitions, your egos, your lives, and follow me into the world of the poor, the world at war. Follow the way of the cross, the way of nonviolent resistance to death. Say No to war and Yes to life."

These four women demonstrate a contemporary practice of solidarity with the poor. They fell in love with the face of God in the face of the poor, so naturally, they were willing to lay down their lives for the poor, for Christ, to suffer the same fate as the poor. "The Church's role is to accompany those who suffer the most, and to witness our hope in the resurrection," wrote Clarke. Ford asked, "The challenge that we live daily is to enter into the paschal mystery with faith. Am I willing to suffer with the people here, the suffering of the powerless?"[9] It follows that just as they died with Christ because of their solidarity with the poor and resistance to evil, so too are they rising with Christ in the new resisting communities that carry on their dream.

These four women resisted death—actively, publicly, provocatively, and at great risk to themselves. They prayed over and picked up the dead bodies of the poor. In resisting death, they defended life. They went to the prisons and got people released. They spoke up to generals, death squad leaders, and U.S. government officials. They lived out the dream of Jesus—they preached good news to the poor, they proclaimed liberty to captives, and they helped the oppressed go free. They lived nonviolent resistance by walking into a war and proclaiming peace with their lives. They loved their nation's enemies by serving the enemy people who suffered under U.S. guns. They pleaded for the lives of their enemies. They had gone to the outskirts of the American "empire" and encountered the results of what Donovan called First World sin: mutilated bodies, poverty, injustice, death.

Living in the United States is like living in the calm eye of a hurricane, the center of the empire; it is hard to see the ravages the violence inflicts upon the poor. Everything appears peaceful. The suffering poor are pushed out of sight. But in Third World countries such as El Salvador, the violence of the imperial hurricane is everywhere. Like any hurricane, it leaves a trail of dead bodies. These four saw this and acted publicly to stop it.

The four churchwomen's discipleship was, by its very nature, illegal.

Most importantly, their resistance took the form of gospel nonviolence. They were nonviolent and consciously chose to be nonviolent. They saw their work with the church as "the only nonviolent voice in the whole country," as Donovan wrote.[10] In El Salvador, their lives were one continuous act of civil disobedience. Jean explained to a friend at one point, "The only crime here in Salvador is being young."[11] She had a youthful view of life and its fullness. Living such a vision of life in today's world defies the death squads and all forces that cut life short. The churchwomen discovered that it was illegal to serve the poor and defend life the way they did. It is illegal to seek justice, to pursue the dream of Jesus in a land of war. No wonder they were killed, just as Jesus was. Their work was illegal and their brutal murders were to be expected. The murders, on the other hand, were legal, just as Jesus' murder was legal, ordered from on high.

After Donovan's death, Pat Donovan, her mother, found a prayer in Jean's Bible that read, "I pray that I will be an example of Christ's love and peace."[12] These women maintained their way of nonviolence in the thick of violence, in the shadow of death. At one point, they considered a violent defense of themselves and their friends; but they rejected those offers in order to be in keeping with the gospel. Just a few months before her death, Donovan told her fiance, Doug Cable, that a friend in Guatemala tried to give her a pistol, but she refused to take it. Cable wrote, "They wanted to be clearly not taking sides in the armed conflict. This was a positive action and not a defense. It was a statement to the many victimized, unarmed civilians that they stood with them. I believe that, in this, the Holy Spirit walked with them all."[13]

To be a person of active nonviolence is to dream great dreams. These women dreamed of a world where people no longer kill one another but where all love one another as Christ loved us. They lived to make that dream come true.

In their struggle to be faithful, to resist death, to witness for peace, to be nonviolent, they were given a deep gift of inner peace—the gift of nonviolence. They became more peaceful with their fate, the fate of the poor. This can be seen particularly in Donovan's life. She was given a deep sense of peace—the gift of the Risen Christ—not in the American business world but among the refugees of Central America.

In death, Jean Donovan, Ita Ford, Maura Clarke, and Dorothy Kazel have become martyrs of the church. God raised them up in the eyes of the poor, and they are a sign to us all, a sign from God, model disciples for Christians in the United States. As Salvadoran theologian Jon Sobrino explains, "In Ita, Maura, Dorothy, and Jean, God has visited El Salvador."[14]

What can we do to honor them? What can we learn from them about being followers of Jesus?

We can become people who dream about the kingdom of God here on earth, people who seek that kingdom with all our hearts. We can resist death here at home. We can take up a preferential option for the poor and a preferential option for peace; that is, to follow Jesus. We can choose to be humble heroes. This is what Jesus, and the four women, lived for, died for, and dreamed of.

The dreamers have been killed and people wait to see what will become of the dream. Many have given up any hope of changing the world into a nonviolent place. The dreamers refused to give up hope and ask us to do likewise.

May we take up their dream of God's kingdom on earth. May we be faithful to it and may the dream become reality.

Notes

1. For further information on the life of Sr. Ita Ford, see Judith Noone, *The Same Fate as the Poor* (Maryknoll, N.Y.: Maryknoll Sisters Publications, 1984); and Donna Whitson Brett and Edward T. Brett, *Murdered in Central America: The Stories of Eleven U.S. Missionaries* (Maryknoll, N.Y.: Orbis Books, 1988).

2. For further information on the life of Sr. Maura Clarke, see Noone, *The Same Fate as the Poor*; and Brett and Brett, *Murdered in Central America*.

3. For further information on the life of Sr. Dorothy Kazel, see Dorothy Chapon Kazel, *Alleluia Woman: Sister Dorothy Kazel, O.S.U.* (Cleveland, Oh.: Chapel Publications, 1987), as well as Brett and Brett, *Murdered in Central America*.

4. For further information on the life of Jean Donovan, see Ana Carrigan, *Salvador Witness: The Life and Calling of Jean Donovan* (New York: Simon & Schuster, 1984); Brett and Brett, *Murdered in Central America*; John Dear, *Jean Donovan: The Call to Discipleship* (Benet Press, 1986; available from Pax Christi USA, 348 East Tenth Street, Erie, PA 16503); and the documentary film, *Roses in December* (available from First Run Features, 153 Waverly Place, New York, N.Y. 10014, (212) 243–0600).

5. The amount of U.S. military aid to El Salvador has increased steadily since the 1970s. It was only halted for a month—after the four women were killed. For further information on U.S. military intervention in El Salvador, contact: The Religious Task Force on Central America, 1747 Connecticut Avenue, N.W., Washington, D.C. 20009; (202) 387–7652; and Going Home/ SHARE, Box 24, Cardinal Station, Washington, D.C. 20064; (202) 635–5540. See also John Dear, "Peace and War in the Land of the Savior," in *El Salvador* (Benet Press, 1987, available from Pax Christi).

6. Carrigan, *Salvador Witness,* 218.

7. From a sermon given on April 1, 1979. In Oscar Romero, *The Violence of Love: The Pastoral Wisdom of Archbishop Oscar Romero,* comp. and ed. James R. Brockman, S.J. (San Francisco: Harper & Row, 1988), 154. For further information on the life of Oscar Romero, see James Brockman, *The Word Remains: A Life of Oscar Romero* (Maryknoll, N.Y.: Orbis Books, 1982).

8. Romero, *The Violence of Love,* 228; and Noone, *Same Fate as the Poor,* 137.

9. Noone, *Same Fate as the Poor,* 87.

10. Carrigan, *Salvador Witness,* 193.

11. Ibid., 46.

12. From conversations between Pat Donovan and the author.

13. Letter from Doug Cable to the author, May 31, 1987.

14. Jon Sobrino, *Spirituality of Liberation: Toward Political Holiness* (Maryknoll, N.Y.: Orbis Books, 1988), 156.

7

Thomas Merton

"THE GOD OF PEACE IS NEVER GLORIFIED BY HUMAN VIOLENCE"

Nineteen sixty-eight was a watershed year of upheaval: the Vietnam War, the deaths of Martin Luther King, Jr., and Robert Kennedy, the Catonsville draft board raid and subsequent trial, the Democratic convention in Chicago, the election of Richard Nixon. Such events formed the setting in which I grew up. I do not remember anything about Thomas Merton, who died in Bangkok on December 10, 1968, at the age of fifty-seven. Yet I see myself as one of his heirs, one whose soul has blossomed and flourished thanks to his prayer, his journey, his life.

When Thomas Merton entered the Trappist monastery of Gethsemani near Louisville, Kentucky, on December 10, 1941, he planned to flee the world and devote his life to prayer. Through the grace of those prayers, he learned, however, to turn to the world and offer everyone the insights and blessings he had gained from his monastic journey.[1] He was a writer, and he began writing poetry, books on contemplation, life, and peace, as well as journals of his daily thoughts and meditations. His autobiography, *The Seven Storey Mountain*, published on July 7, 1948, became a national best seller. Through the 1950s and 1960s, other significant works of his appeared—*The Sign of Jonas, The Waters of Siloe, New Seeds of Contemplation, Seeds of Destruction, Faith and Violence*, and *Conjectures of a Guilty Bystander*. As Merton became an outspoken opponent of war and nuclear weapons and a teacher of nonviolence, he offered the insight that true peacemaking is a spiritual matter. He maintained that nonviolence requires prayer and the purity of heart that comes from a contemplative life. He called his readers and friends to nourish the roots of our spiritual lives in God if we are to undertake the life work of peacemaking and nonviolent resistance to injustice and war. He encouraged us to seek reality and celebrate life, even as we struggle to defend it. As antiwar activists and resisters were to discover, Merton's message was very important.

On the final page of *The Seven Storey Mountain*, Merton writes that he hears God speaking to him: "I will give you what you desire. I will lead you into solitude. . . . And your solitude will bear immense fruit in the souls of men and women you will never see on earth."[2] The solitude and the nonviolence of Thomas Merton have borne immense fruit in the soul of this Christian, and, I know, in many others'.

Merton lived up to the expectations he himself prophesied in the final pages of *The Seven Storey Mountain*. He wrote of "learning to know the Christ of the burnt men [and women]." On his final journey, a pilgrimage to Asia, he wrote in his journal that he experienced the emptiness and compassion of Christ in new ways as he stood before the Buddhas of Polonarruwa. Then, after speaking to monks from around the world, he died, accidentally electrocuted by an old fan. He was burnt physically, and, through a lifetime of prayer and searching, he was burnt spiritually as well, purified by God, so that he became, as he had hoped, "the brother of God."[3]

Merton's life of prayer, contemplation, and solitude, as well as his intensive writing agenda, led him to experience deep freedom. His simple goal was to live in reality, to be aware of other people as children of God, to care for the environment (which he did at the monastery), to transform his own inner violence into peace through prayer so that others could learn from him. He sought to lose himself in the spirit of God and, in the process, to lead others to the spirit of God. His liberation bore tremendous fruit. He spoke to the world as the prophets of old had done, addressing serious issues with the most compassionate tone, the most human voice. He did not join in civil rights and antiwar protests during the 1960s (though his name was often used to support and sponsor antiwar groups), but instead focused his life on a determined resistance to the roots of violence, and was thus focused on commitment to the roots of nonviolence. He became a prophet within the peace movement, calling people to remain pure in heart, at peace within themselves, steadfast in their struggle toward a nonviolent spirit. He was the parish priest of the peace movement, as one friend of his later wrote. Dedicated to poverty, chastity, and obedience in community and prayer, a hermit for the kingdom's sake, Merton proclaimed to the mountaintops: "No more nuclear war! No more injustice! The God of peace is never glorified by human violence. Let us live together as the brothers and sisters that we are." Merton explored life as a way of nonviolence. As he spoke out against the forces of death, he lived and breathed deeply the beauty of life.

Merton's approach to nonviolence is clearly expressed in his confessional essay "The Day of a Stranger," written with the humor that his best friends would recognize. He describes the valley that lay before his hermitage and he notes the SAC planes that flew directly over him carrying nuclear weapons. And he describes his day: "What I wear is pants. What I do is live. How I pray is breathe. Up here in the woods is seen the New Testament: that is to say, the wind comes through the trees and you breathe it."[4] He goes up to the monastery, where he speaks to the novices. He returns to the woods, where he is "a nobody," experiencing the ground zero of humility that Gandhi described. The nobodyness, the loss of his self in the spirit of God, was a gift Merton consciously and deliberately offered to the world, particularly to Christians living in the United States. But losing his life amidst the solitude of a long Kentucky loneliness was not accomplished without paying a price. Merton gave up his own ambitions, goals, worldly desires, possessions, and all the trappings of American culture. He paid that price, with sweat and tears, and offered the world the fruit of his suffering: a word of peace, a word of contemplation. In an age of nuclear weapons and war, he showed Americans how to be human.

Merton's *kenosis* set forth a fire in the church. Here was this monk, famous for leaving the world and its sin, retiring to a life of silence, speaking loudly and boldly to that world with a great spirit of love for one and all. He lived and breathed the spirit of nonviolence, hoping that others too would catch the lightning fires of Pentecostal nonviolence. His trip to Asia, as activist-theologian Jim Douglass has pointed out, was an effort to investigate what Merton called "an ontology of nonviolence." Merton searched for that ontology in his own heart. He studied the threat of nuclear and conventional warfare and posed an unlikely but very Christian question: "If we want to end war, hadn't we best begin by ending the wars in our own hearts?"

When Merton participated in a conference in Calcutta in the fall of 1968, he was asked to lead the closing prayer. He asked the participants to join hands and to become aware of "the love that unites us, the love that unites us in spite of real differences, real emotional friction. The things that are on the surface are nothing, what is deep is the Real. We are creatures of love."[5]

His prayer reflected this reality, a truth that was the fruit of his nonviolent, contemplative life: "Oh God, we are one with You. . . . You have taught us that if we are open to one another, You dwell in us. . . . Help us to preserve this openness and to fight for it with all our hearts. Help us to realize that there can be no understanding where there is mutual rejection. Oh God, in accepting one another wholeheartedly, fully, completely, we accept You, and we thank You, and we adore You, and we love You with our whole being, because our being is in Your being, our spirit is rooted in Your Spirit. Fill us then with love, and let us be bound together with love as we go our diverse ways, united in this one spirit which makes You present in the world. . . ."[6]

In his essay "The Root of War Is Fear," Merton passionately urged all Christians to work for the peace that already unites us in reality, which God has already granted to us, which already makes us brothers and sisters of one another, children of God. We have to work to help each other become aware of the reality of who we are, God's very own children. "What are we to do?" he asked. "The duty of the Christian in this crisis is to strive with all [her] power and intelligence, with [her] faith, [her] hope in Christ, and love for God and humanity, to do the one task which God has imposed upon us in the world today. That task is to work for the total abolition of war. There can be no question that unless war is abolished the world will remain constantly in a state of madness and desperation in which, because of the immense destructive power of modern weapons, the danger of catastrophe will be imminent and probable at every moment everywhere."[7]

His message summoned one and all to join the struggle for peace that breaks beyond political barriers, into what he termed "the human dimension." He wanted all of us to share in "the happiness of being at one with everything in that hidden ground of Love for which there can be no explanations." Merton pointed to the unity underlying humanity's divisions. "What is important in nonviolence," he wrote, "is the contemplative truth that is not seen. The radical truth of reality is that we are all one."[8]

Merton's language was strong; his tone peaceful, but urgent. He wrote as a messenger from the desert, with a voice crying out in the wilderness of America. His plea to Christians involved a radical reorientation of goals—to make peacemaking the heart of our ministry.

The church must lead the way on the road to nonviolent settlement of difficulties and toward the gradual abolition of war as the way of settling international or civil disputes. Christians must become active in every possible way, mobilizing all their resources for the fight against war. . . . Peace is to be preached, nonviolence is to be explained as a practical method, and not left to be mocked as an outlet for crackpots who want to make a show of themselves. Prayer and sacrifice must be used as the most effective spiritual weapons in the war against war, and like all weapons, they must be used with deliberate aim: not just with a vague aspiration for peace and security, but against violence and war. This implies that we are also willing to sacrifice and restrain our own instinct for violence and aggressiveness in our relations with other people. We may never succeed in this campaign, but whether we succeed or not, the duty is evident. It is the great Christian task of our time. Everything else is secondary, for the survival of the human race itself depends upon it."[9]

Merton sought to live his faith with intensity and simplicity. He wrote, "It is my intention to make my entire life a rejection of, a protest against, the crimes and injustices of war and political tyranny which threaten to destroy the whole human race and the world."[10] While his monastic life was a protest against human violence, his life of silence and contemplation was also a "yes to all that is good in the world and in humanity . . . to all that is beautiful in nature."

Merton's essay "Blessed Are the Meek: The Christian Roots of Nonviolence" is essential reading for all people committed to the gospel struggle for peace with justice. "The chief difference between violence and nonviolence," he explained, "is that violence depends entirely on its own calculations. Nonviolence depends entirely on God and God's Word."[11]

Merton identified seven biblical, theological "conditions for relative honesty in the practice of Christian nonviolence." They are as timely and in need of study today as the day he wrote them.[12]

1. Nonviolence must be aimed above all at the transformation of the present state of the world. It must therefore be free even from the unconscious yet unjust use of power.

2. The nonviolent resistance of Christians who belong to one of the powerful nations and who are themselves in some sense privileged members of world society will have to be done clearly not for themselves but for others, that is, for the poor and underprivileged.

3. In the nonviolent struggle for peace, the threat of nuclear war abolishes all privilege. Thus, nonviolence must not be ambiguously advocated or practiced via unclear and confusing protests that can harden warmakers in their self-righteous blindness. Nonviolent resisters must avoid a similar facile and fanatical self-righteousness, and must refrain from being satisfied with dramatic self-justifying gestures.

4. The most insidious temptation to be avoided is the desire for immediate visible results. The Christian humility of nonviolent action must establish itself in the minds and memories of modern humanity not only as *conceivable and possible,* but as *a desirable alternative* [Merton's emphasis] to what people now consider the only realistic possibility, namely, political technique backed by force.

5. The manner in which the conflict for truth is waged will itself manifest or obscure the truth. To fight for truth by dishonest, violent, inhuman, or unreasonable means would simply betray

the truth one is trying to vindicate. The absolute refusal of evil or suspect means is a necessary element in the witness of nonviolence.

6. Nonviolent resisters should be willing to learn something from their adversaries. "If a new truth is made known to us by or through the adversary, will we accept it? Are we willing to admit that he is not totally inhumane, wrong, unreasonable, and cruel?" he asked.

7. Christian hope and Christian humility are inseparable. The quality of our nonviolence is decided largely by the purity of the Christian hope behind it.

Merton was able to reflect so deeply on the truth of nonviolence because he first lived it to the depths in his monastic life. He spent his days in prayer, work, and reflection; and he spoke out against racism, the Vietnam war, and nuclear war. These prophetic insights were not well accepted by his monastic community, and he suffered for seeking and speaking the truth. He refused to participate in a life that pretended to be religious but that ignored the reality of death in the world: war and the nuclear threat. He wrote to a friend,

In this situation of nuclear danger, I have thought that it would be a matter of fidelity to my vocation as a Christian and a priest, and by no means in contradiction to my state as monk, to try to show clearly that our advance toward nuclear war is morally intolerable and even criminal, and that we have to take the most serious possible steps to realize our condition and do something about it.[13]

Merton's monastic vocation of prayer and writing called for a complete dissociation from the violent life, the frenzied life of disorientation and evil. Merton taught that peacemaking goes hand in hand with contemplation. One can sustain a life of nonviolent love and active resistance in America, Merton repeated, only through regular prayer and resting in the peace of God. Until his death, Merton continued to examine these two poles of the Christian life and to unite them in himself. Through his explorations in Zen Buddhism, Merton sought to empty himself as Christ did, letting go of his ego and taking up the cross of love so that Christ could live in him. His search for truth via

Eastern spirituality led him to let go of power and ego, in the being of Christ, the spirit of nonviolence, the unity of humanity—love.

In the solitude of the hermitage, Merton pursued depths of inner freedom through the nonviolence and resistance of contemplative love and prophetic writing. From his experience of liberation, he spoke to the world about a way of liberation and life—the way of the cross, the way of nonviolent resistance. He was able to show the way to others who were actively involved in the struggle for justice and peace, helping them remain focused on the ultimate reward. In one of his final talks, in Calcutta, he concluded: "My brothers and sisters, we are already one. But we imagine that we are not. And what we have to recover is our original unity. What we have to be is what we are."[14]

The God of peace was glorified in the peacemaking life of Thomas Merton. Perhaps the best way to remember Merton is to commit ourselves to the life of nonviolent love he endeavored to live, taking courage in his example, and going to the roots of contemplative love as an act of resistance to war in our own hearts and in our world.

Notes

1. For a complete and thorough study of the life of Thomas Merton, read Michael Mott, *The Seven Mountains of Thomas Merton* (Boston: Houghton Mifflin, 1984). See also James Forest, *Thomas Merton: A Pictorial Biography* (Mahwah, N.J.: Paulist Press, 1984); Thomas P. McDonnell, ed., *A Thomas Merton Reader* (New York: Image Books, 1974); Gordan Zahn, ed., *The Nonviolent Alternative* (New York: Farrar, Straus & Giroux, 1980); Patrick Hart, ed., *Thomas Merton/Monk: A Monastic Tribute* (Kalamazoo, Mich.: Cistercian Publications, 1983); William H. Shannon, ed., *The Hidden Ground of Love: The Letters of Thomas Merton,* vol. 1 (New York: Farrar, Straus & Giroux, 1985); Robert Daggy, ed., *The Road to Joy: The Letters of Thomas Merton,* vol. 2 (New York: Farrar, Straus & Giroux, 1989).

2. McDonnell, *Thomas Merton Reader,* 514–16.

3. Ibid.

4. Ibid., 431–38.

5. *The Asian Journal of Thomas Merton* (New York: New Dimensions, 1975), 318.

6. Ibid., 318–19.

7. Jim Forest, *Thomas Merton's Struggle with Peacemaking* (Erie, Pa.: Benet Press, 1980), 8–9.

8. Ibid., 29.

9. Ibid., 9.

10. Ibid., 21–22.

11. Thomas Merton, "Blessed Are the Meek: The Christian Roots of Nonviolence," in Gordon, ed., *The Nonviolent Alternative*, 209–10.

12. Ibid., 212–16.

13. Daniel Berrigan, "The Peacemaker," in Hart, ed., *Thomas Merton/Monk*, 223.

14. Shannon, ed., *The Hidden Ground of Love*, x.

8

James Douglass

"CHRIST IS RISEN FROM NUCLEAR HOLOCAUST"

Stepping outside his small house by the Naval Submarine Base near Bangor, Washington, the home of the Trident nuclear submarine fleet, Jim Douglass saw an all-white armored train passing before his eyes into the military base. The so-called White Train typically carried between one hundred and two hundred hydrogen bombs. It had traveled, undetected, back and forth, from Amarillo, Texas (the final assembly point for all U.S. nuclear warheads), to Bangor since the early 1960s. The White Train, Jim Douglass wrote, "is the most concentrated symbol we have of the hell of nuclear war."[1] Led and inspired by Douglass and his community, hundreds of people held vigils along the train tracks shortly thereafter, sharing both a vision of love toward the people on the trains and nonviolent resistance to their nuclear cargoes.

Douglass has been actively involved in the antinuclear and peace movements for over thirty years. An author, theologian, university professor, and peace activist, Douglass has consciously sought to live out the gospel mandate of nonviolent love through steadfast resistance to the arms race. In 1976, with his wife, Shelley Douglass, he founded the Ground Zero Center for Nonviolent Action in Bangor, Washington, in order to conduct a nonviolent campaign against the nearby Trident Submarine base. As an experiment in truth and resistance modeled on Gandhi's ashram, Ground Zero perhaps is the best example of a Christian base community of nonviolent resistance to evil in the United States. It follows strictly Gandhi's guidelines for a satyagraha campaign through gospel nonviolence, *agape,* and truthseeking. Through regular leaflets, vigils, and dialogue, community members reach out to military employees at the base and throughout the region. They seek ways to demonstrate love and respect for the workers as human beings, while they try to close the Trident base and all such places. Prayer, fasting, solitude, civil disobedience, simple life style, and community meetings form the unique, full-time campaign of nonviolent love—indeed, a way of life—focused on the Trident base.

Douglass writes,

The White Train can be stopped through education, reflection and prayerful, nonviolent direct action: prayer vigils by the tracks, loving disobedience on the tracks, until there are more people on the tracks prepared to go to jail for peace than there are people to remove them or jails to contain them. Critical to this vision of stopping the White Train is a transforming loving, agape, realized through prayer. . . . What we seek through agape is the conversion of ourselves, through the love of God transforming our hearts, so that we might realize a vision of active, contemplative peacemaking.[2]

The work of Ground Zero is an effort of transformation that begins in the members themselves and reaches out to include the people working on Trident, as Douglass explains:

Trident is dependent on the acceptance, silence, and complicity of the many people in our Pacific area. We live next to the nuclear final solution, the ultimate first strike weapon. . . . We believe Trident can be stopped if we are willing to experiment in the truth of nonviolence and give our lives for it. Trident can be stopped if we can speak the truth over and over again that workers on the Trident base are good people whom we respect and that the weapons system they and we are complicit in building is the Auschwitz of Puget Sound. The truth which has to be realized consists of both of these: good people and the inconceivable evil of Trident—an evil which can then be stopped.

Trident can be stopped if we can realize that all of us, on both sides of the fence and the world, are one in God's love, in the humanity we share and are on the verge of annihilating. We can realize our unity in a process of truth and love which Jesus called "the kingdom of God" and Gandhi called "satyagraha" or "truth-force." The Trident campaign is an experiment in the truth-force of God's kingdom here and now, in our midst—a force of truth and love more powerful than the hydrogen bomb.[3]

In July 1981, Jim and Shelley Douglass and the members of Ground Zero held a retreat along the tracks that entered the submarine base and decided with their network of friends to begin the Agape Community, which would monitor and oppose missile motor shipments. Each person made the following commitment:

1. I commit myself to this community of people and to an agape-based campaign against the shipment of Trident parts.
2. I commit myself to regular fasting and prayer for peace with the community on Mondays.
3. I commit myself to the communal search for God's will in this matter; to give and accept insight, reflection, and correction, and to make decisions based on the leading of the Spirit.
4. I commit myself to a campaign of education, action, and civil disobedience against the shipment of missile parts. I will be open to the will of God in this campaign as we can best discern it together.
5. I commit myself to the transforming power of agape in all aspects of my life, and to nonviolence as an expression of agape in our world.[4]

Since the early 1980s, the Agape Community has tracked down the White Train, held vigils when it passed, and knelt in its path. Hundreds of people from Washington state to Texas and elsewhere have been arrested and jailed for stopping the train. These actions have alerted the public to the nuclear cargoes that have been crisscrossing the country. In an effort to witness to the transforming power of nonviolent love, these new peace communities along the tracks have attempted to reach out and touch those people who work on the train. "We have to stop this White Train to hell," Jim Douglass has written, "but we can stop it only through a truthful, loving process which affirms the sacredness of that life within it."[5] Within two years of the start of the protests, the Department of Energy repainted the nuclear train a mixture of black, green, and brown, similar to army fatigues. Following the motto, "Love will stop the train: Accept Responsibility," Ground Zero continues its nonviolent resistance to nuclear war through acts of public active love. Its members see their struggle as a patient work that will continue for the rest of their lives.

Since the early 1960s, Douglass has been writing about nonviolent resistance while also living it. He maintains that life today is lived to the fullest when one shares the suffering of the poor by resisting evil in a spirit of nonviolent love. His classic work, *The Nonviolent Cross,* begins with the words, "To see reality in our time is to see the world as crucifixion."[6] The cross as the way of nonviolent resistance and the revolution of resurrection form the basis of Douglass's theology, his understanding of the gospel.

Suffering love is the way of the nonviolent Christ, who for Douglass is nothing less than the image of a nonviolent God. God is present in the sufferings of the oppressed and in their risings, through the liberation of active love, as Douglass explains:

The presence of God in humankind is, above all, the presence of humanity crucified. It is a presence dimly seen and scarcely felt when the crucified of humanity are crowded out into the margin of the earth. God lives where men and women are beaten and die, but God lives to bring them and their murderers to life, and God's life comes to life only when God emerges from them as Truth and as Love. The life of God is the life of the crucified, but while God is deeply present in crucifixion, the unveiling of God's presence is in resurrection, a resurrection which can be seen and felt only by those in whom Love and Truth have taken hold. God is dead where men and women lie dying and unseen. God lives where crucifixion is seen and felt and entered into, as neither victim nor executioner but as Love suffering and as Truth overcoming. Crucifixion becomes redemptive precisely when the victim recognizes his or her divinity. Men and women take that step when they respond to injustice with Love: suffering, resistant, and overpowering. Humanity becomes God when Love and Truth enter into humanity, not by humanity's power but by raising humanity to

Power, so that revolution in Love is revealed finally as the Power of resurrection.[7]

The central figure of Truth and Love in nonviolent resistance, Douglass writes, is Jesus of Nazareth, the *ebed Yahweh* of scripture. Through the sufferings of Christ, reenacted today in history, God redeems and transforms injustice into justice, a divided community into a beloved community, damnation into salvation:

To recognize the humanity of the Christ of the cross is to recognize all men and women in him, who in his suffering is one with all those by whom he has been murdered. To pass over to the suffering servanthood of the human Jesus is to see, through his forgiveness, his redeeming presence in all men and women, oppressed and oppressors alike, and to see therefore the possibility of his redeeming mediation through suffering love any human conflict. To profess a living faith in the Christ of the cross is to affirm the redemptive reality present in every cross of suffering love enacted in history. Christ becomes present everywhere as he was present: in suffering servanthood and crucifixion. In and through this presence he redeems humankind from division and leads it into community.[8]

Douglass's God is active in the suffering love of people who resist all that kills and destroys life. His theology of resistance and liberation through nonviolence is developed further in his book *Resistance and Contemplation: The Way of Liberation.* "A way of liberation passes through fire because the only God who has been known to liberate is the God who continually suffers and dies in humanity out of love for the people."[9] Liberation occurs through nonviolence, when powerlessness is accepted and the power of God is allowed to work in one's spirit of love and truth.

Nonviolent liberation seeks the redemption of humanity from power itself, from all power *over* men and women, which is a power of domination and sin. The only power nonviolent liberation seeks is a power for human beings—the power to serve, to care, to love, to build the earth into a city of brothers and sisters, after the example of the God who loved and served humanity to the point of making himself powerless. . . . To the revolutionary of the Kingdom, liberation will mean finally the disappearance of all power over people in the new reality of the human family's communion with the God of Love. The Gospel suggests that the way to realize that vision is to live it now in its fullness. A way of liberation discovered through the Gospel will have its roots and its power in an almost forgotten faith, a faith of crucifixion and resurrection, a faith of scandalous death and joyful life. Jesus was only one of thousands of Jewish revolutionaries executed on Roman crosses. At the time of his death, one needed faith to believe that anything good or joyful could come from a cross. The faith of the cross is no less a scandal today, and no less powerful in giving strength to the few who take it seriously.[10]

The way of liberation is a way of resistance and contemplation, Douglass suggests. "In resisting the system, I resist out of my own powerlessness, and my sense of powerlessness deepens with my commitment of resistance."[11] *Kenosis*, the accepted powerlessness of Christ, is the fruit of contemplation and resistance. It is a powerlessness that gets deeper and deeper in the power of Love and Truth that resists evil. This insight has become one of the central points of Douglass's theology of nonviolent resistance and Ground Zero's discoveries. In Gandhi's terminology, this lifework of self-emptying meant "having nothing to do with power" and "reducing one's self to zero." "To reduce oneself completely to zero in the struggle for a universally compassionate truth," Douglass has written, "would be to set off an explosion in the world which would be as powerful spiritually as the atomic bomb was materially."[12]

By letting go of ourselves in the way of liberation, Douglass explains, nonviolent resisters must let go of the drive to be effective. "The way of effectiveness runs counter to liberation," he states, as Thomas Merton also realized. The philosophy of calculation and technique is ultimately destructive and self-defeating. By *not* trying to be effective, but by being faithful to the way of nonviolent resistance, one experiences the liberation one seeks.[13]   The voluntary acceptance of arrest, trial, prison, suffering, and death become then part of the way of nonviolent resistance as liberation. These avenues lead to freedom—for oneself and for others—the freedom that is resurrection and God's own peace.

The God (of Jesus) . . . is a God of Liberation—and of such radical liberation that God wages a permanent revolution down through history against every kingdom and state in existence—a revolution to liberate *all* the oppressed, free *all* the prisoners, give back land to *all* people—a revolution to set everyone free, to level all corporate and bureaucratic power, to break open the prisons, to smash every war machine known to humanity, and to do so without swearing allegiance to a single regime or ideology in history, for God the Liberator is alone to be worshipped, God the Condemned and Executed and Always Resurrected—the enemy of every state—is alone to be served.[14]

Just as Jesus and Gandhi experimented in truth, so, too, Jim Douglass and the Ground Zero resisters are experimenting in the truth of nonviolence at the very place of the greatest force of violence in the history of the world. The life campaign of nonviolent resistance begun by Jim and Shelley Douglass and the Ground Zero community has involved many actions of nonviolent civil disobedience and much time in prison for their steadfast witness. Through years of reflection on active nonviolence, Douglass has come to see the experience of jail as a time of monastic prayer for peace. This insight is a peculiarly American understanding of nonviolent resistance as a theology of liberation:

In a society preparing for nuclear war and ignoring its poor, jail is an appropriate setting in which to give one's life to prayer. In a nation which has legalized preparations for the destruction of all life on earth, going to jail for peace—through nonviolent civil disobedience—can be seen as a prayer. In reflecting today on the Lord's Prayer, I think that going to jail as a way of saying "thy kingdom come, thy will be done" may be the most basic prayer we can offer in the nuclear security state. . . . As members of such a nation, we need to pray for the freedom to do God's will by non-cooperating with the ultimate evil it is preparing. Civil disobedience done in a loving spirit is itself that kind of prayer.[15]

"For socially powerless people nonviolent civil disobedience can be a profoundly liberating way out of bondage, as one part of a larger revolution," Douglass continues. This resistance is not a method of ego-empowerment but a self-emptying process that publicly says no to the evil of nuclear weapons.

Our God Is Nonviolent

To live out the kingdom of God through such an action is to live in a loving relationship to our brothers and sisters in the police, in courts, and in jails, recognizing God's presence in each of us. It is also to accept responsibility for an evil which is ours: As we are, so is the nuclear state. . . . I believe that a suffering God continually calls us to be in such places for the sake of peace and justice. I believe that the kingdom of God is realized there. Civil disobedience as prayer is a way into that kingdom.[16]

Jim Douglass and the Ground Zero Community of Bangor, Washington, have gone deep into the powerlessness of active nonviolent resistance against the nuclear arms race, in the tradition of King, Merton, Day, Gandhi, and other prophets of nonviolence. They have been able to do so because of the examples of those apostles who have gone before them. They have attempted to apply the lessons of nonviolence at the sight of terrible violence, in order to reveal God's power of nonviolent love. They have focused their energies and lives on the transforming power of God's love in them when they dedicate themselves to nonviolent resistance at a Trident submarine base. Their living struggle continues today. While history awaits the revelation of that transforming love, they know and act on the truth that it has already begun.

Douglass has emerged as one of the leading actors and thinkers in the Christian movement for peace in the United States. His life and theology continue to bear fruit for the liberation of many.

Douglass's good news of nonviolent resistance is simple, yet it is a message that speaks directly to the truth of American culture: "Jesus' death and resurrection today open up the process and possibility of a new humanity through which divine love can transform history into a nuclear-free world. We can live in faith so that Christ in us is risen from nuclear holocaust. Jesus' resurrection and the inconceivable growth of his band of disciples are testimony to the Christian in the nuclear age that for God anything is possible within history, but only through the total gift of our lives."[17]

Notes

1. James Douglass, "The Nuclear Train Campaign: Tracking and Resisting the Train," in Jim Wallis, ed., *The Rise of Christian Conscience* (San Francisco: Harper & Row, 1987), 66.

2. Ibid., 71.

3. Ibid.

4. James Douglass, "All Along the Tracks," *Ground Zero* (April/May 1983): 2.

5. Douglass, "Nuclear Train Campaign," in Wallis, ed, *The Rise of Christian Conscience,* 64.

6. James Douglass, *The Nonviolent Cross: A Theology of Revolution and Peace* (New York: Macmillan Co., 1968), 3.

7. Ibid., 23–24.

8. Ibid., 72–73.

9. James Douglass, *Resistance and Contemplation: The Way of Liberation* (New York: Doubleday & Co., 1972), 25.

10. Ibid., 43–44.

11. Ibid., 141–42.

12. Ibid., 145–46.

13. Ibid., 179–80.

14. Ibid., 77.

15. James Douglass, "Civil Disobedience as a Way of Prayer" in Arthur Laffin and Anne Montgomery, eds., *Swords into Plowshares: Nonviolent Direct Action for Disarmament* (San Francisco: Harper & Row, 1987), 93.

16. Ibid., 96–97.

17. James Douglass, "Christ Is Risen from Nuclear Holocaust," in Jim Wallis, ed., *Waging Peace* (San Francisco: Harper & Row, 1982), 250. For further information on the work of Ground Zero and to receive their newsletter, *Ground Zero,* write to: Ground Zero, 16159 Clear Creek Road, N.W., Poulsbo, WA, 98370.

9

Daniel Berrigan

"WE MUST NOT KILL IF
WE ARE CHRISTIANS"

In the early 1980s, when I first contemplated taking part in an act of nonviolent civil disobedience at the Pentagon, I attended a retreat with Jesuit Father Daniel Berrigan in the hills of northeastern Pennsylvania. As we sat up talking late one night, I shared with him both my desire to get involved in the Christian peace movement and the call I felt to join those who were resisting the nuclear arms race by sitting-in at places such as the Pentagon. One factor was holding me back, I confessed. I was afraid. I was afraid of the reaction from my family and friends. I was concerned about how this step would change my life, presumably forever.

His response was simple yet very profound. It was straight from the gospel. "Do not be afraid. Take the risk and trust in God. This is what our Christianity is all about."

Daniel Berrigan has been inspiring Christians across the country, indeed, around the world, with that gospel message of risk taking and truth telling. His words and the example of his life have demonstrated how the gospel is to be lived in the nuclear age: through steadfast nonviolent resistance to injustice and the forces of death. As a longtime peace activist, author, poet, and theologian, Berrigan has emerged as the foremost proponent of nonviolence and resistance in the United States today. He has become, as Martin Luther King, Jr., became for the civil rights movement, a roving preacher and protagonist for a nuclear-free, nonviolent world. Although he would object to the label, he has become a prophet to the nation, a sort of free-lance resister, challenging the American people to become a people of justice and mercy, and not vengeance and violence. A gentle, peaceful, quiet person, he has dedicated his life to breaking our culture's addiction to death.

For the last thirty years, Berrigan has committed himself to the cause of peace with justice. By traveling the nation and the world, reflecting on the gospel and scriptures, writing hundreds of poems, essays, and over thirty-five books, standing with the marginalized, and demonstrating against war, Berrigan has lived a deep discipleship to Christ and witnessed to the truth of Christ's nonviolent love. Through countless nonviolent actions, arrests, and years in prison, Berrigan has remained faithful to the gospel vision of Christ as a nonviolent, loving resister. He has taken the call to choose life seriously by resisting death and the metaphors of death that plague humanity. From the crucified and risen Christ, Berrigan finds the strength to walk fearlessly and freely to those places of death in order to bring light. Berrigan remains a living sign of hope amidst a despairing nation: he refuses to give in to the world of death and war. He continues to stand up (or sit down) for truth and love. In his witness against all forms of death, whether abortion, capital punishment, war, or the nuclear arms race, Berrigan's biblical message stays the same: We are not allowed to kill. In the nuclear age, such a message is considered by some to be subversive. From the perspective of the law, putting such a belief into practice is illegal. But Berrigan has come to see the urgent duty of peacemaking not just as the necessary step for survival, but as the very definition of Christianity. To be a Christian for Berrigan is to be a peacemaker, a nonviolent resister, one who turns over the tables of injustice, one who follows the illegal, resisting, dangerous, loving Jesus.

"Our real shrines are nuclear installations and the Pentagon and the war research laboratories," he writes about our culture. "This is where we worship, allowing ourselves to hear the obscene command that we kill and be killed—a command which, it seems to me, is anti-Christ, anti-God. The mainline churches have joined this effort to make killing acceptable and normal—at least by silence."[1] The command that follows is clear: "No killing, no war, which is to say, above all, no nuclear weapons. And thence the imperative: Resist those who research, deploy or justify, on whatever grounds, such weaponry."[2]

Berrigan says that "death is a social method, a disease; violence is the public method."[3] Berrigan calls the world "the kingdom of death, where everything is meshing and dying." Into this world, he explains, arrives the great yes of God, the Christ, "bringing trouble and all sorts of dislocations, unmasking, lawbreaking, truthtelling." Berrigan preaches "the great scandal of history: the disarmed God and the disarming of God in Christ." Christ the dislocator does "the wrong things, in the wrong places, at the wrong time, to the wrong people."[4] Jesus comes healing, reconciling, bringing truth, deliberately creating scenes, practicing nonviolent loving disobedience everywhere. In a similar manner, the Christian is personally disarmed, healed and healing, reconciling in today's world, doing the wrong things, in the wrong places, at the wrong times, to the wrong people, and paying the penalty for such disturbing activity. "We are being asked to live out the drama of the disarmed Christ in a world armed to the teeth. To confess Jesu these days is to be working for peace."[5]

With this image of Jesus as the great upsetter who turns the tables on the kingdom of death by bringing life, breaking unjust laws, and dislocating demonic structures, Daniel Berrigan strives to be a faithful disciple aware of the realities of our times. Berrigan has been arrested repeatedly since his first arrest at an anti–Vietnam war rally at the Pentagon in 1967. The most famous of his acts of resistance were the burning of draft records in the Catonsville Nine action of May 19, 1968, and the Plowshares Eight action of September 9, 1980, in which nuclear warheads were hammered on. With Philip Berrigan and Elizabeth McAlister and other family members, he continues the work of nonviolent resistance today.

At the center of his resistance is a deep commitment to nonviolence, as he described in his autobiography, *To Dwell in Peace*:

Nonviolence first and foremost, with its fiery trail of implication: compassion for the adversary, care of one another, community discipline, prayer and sacrament and biblical literacy. Long-term carefulness and short, care of little matters and large, the short run and the long. It was easy to set down a formula and devilishly hard to live by it, even in minor matters. We had to discover such things for ourselves by reading the lives of the saints, pondering their secrets and spirit and tactic; what they had come on, what accomplished; the place of trial and error, that great winnower and humiliator. And by pondering the gospel. And by listening to one another, and talking. But listening more than talking, a rare proportion and difficult to honor.[6]

The Catonsville action caught the attention of the nation and spurred people to more active resistance of the war in southeast Asia. Although the war was long in ending, such actions had an impact on its conclusion. The burning of draft files at Catonsville helped to prevent the U.S. government from using nuclear weapons on the Vietnamese people. Catonsville, Berrigan reflected later, "was like a firebreak, a small fire lit to contain and conquer a greater. . . . Catonsville seemed to light up the dark places of the heart where courage and risk and hope were awaiting a signal, a dawn."[7]

Berrigan emerged from two years in the Danbury, Connecticut, prison with a renewed zeal for peace, aimed pointedly at reversing the nuclear arms race. The Plowshares Eight antinuclear protest in King of Prussia, Pennsylvania, set the pace for a new kind of resistance in the nuclear age. At the trial of the eight, Berrigan related his reason for "doing what is right because it is right":

We could not not do this. We were pushed to this by all our lives. . . . With every cowardly bone in my body I wished I hadn't had to enter the G.E. plant. I wish I hadn't had to do it. And that has been true every time I have been arrested, all those years. My stomach turns over. I feel sick. I feel afraid. I don't want to go through this again. I hate jail. I don't do well there physically. But I cannot not go on, because I have learned that we must not kill if we are Christians. I have learned that children, above all, are threatened by these weapons. I have read that Christ our Lord underwent death rather than inflict it. And I am supposed to be a disciple.[8]

The deepest meaning of the Plowshares Eight action, he explained to members of his Jesuit community, broke beyond "all ideologies, tactics, or plenary punishments meted out to us. . . . We wanted to taste the resurrection. We wanted to taste the resurrection in our bones; to see if we might live in hope, instead of nuclear despair. . . . May I say we have not been disappointed."[9]

A deep belief in the resurrection of Jesus is central to Berrigan's committed life of nonviolent resistance. His summary of the gospel message sums up his theology and the source of his strength.

Once there was a dead man, a criminal, a subject of capital punishment. And lo! he refused to stay dead. He stood up. As the authorities shortly came to sense, this was an earthquake in nature; in the nature of law and order, in the nature of death, the nature of war. For in the nature of things, as defined by the nation state (a great one for deciding what the nature of things is)—dead men stay dead. The word from Big Brother, the word that gives him clout, inspires fear, is—A criminal, once disposed of, stays disposed!

Not at all; along come these crazies shouting in public, "Our man's not dead, He's risen!" Now I submit you can't have such a word going around, and still run the state properly. The first nonviolent revolution was, of course, the Resurrection. The event had to include death as its first act. And also the command to Peter, "Put up your sword." So that it might be clear, once and for all, that Christians suffer death rather than inflict it.[10]

Berrigan's hopeful activity for peace is fundamentally rooted in the resurrection and what that means for us today, as he has explained:

"Witness of the resurrection" was the self-conferred title of honor of the early Twelve. It meant they stood by life, to the point of undergoing death, as well as death's analogous punishments; floggings, scorn, jail. Their understanding was: where there could be no debate, there could be no combat. This is our glory, from Peter and Paul to Martin King and Romero. We know how to live and how to die.[11]

Berrigan's life of resistance has also been rooted in the tradition of prayer, spiritual discernment, solidarity with the poor and dying, and a deep meditation and study of the scriptures. Berrigan draws upon the springs of nonviolence and resistance in Isaiah and the prophets, the Psalms, the Gospels, Paul's prison letters, and the book of Revelation. In many ways, Berrigan's public witness continues the early acts of the apostles. He works to build and support communities of nonviolent resistance like those early Christian communities, to go with fellow Christians into the streets of our cities and talk with people about the good news of peace, and to offer a consistent No to the crimes of the age.

As the early Christians were healed by Jesus and then went out to heal others, Berrigan suggests that today's public work of nonviolent resistance is a new manifestation of the ancient Christian ministry of healing. "We are really trying to heal people, heal a culture, heal the Pentagon, and heal where we are."[12] The great gift of Jesus' healing work of peacemaking was the gift of his life on the cross, Berrigan points out. The price of peacemaking, of nonviolent resistance, is the body and blood of Jesus, given over for the reconciliation of all. Nonviolent resistance for peace with justice requires the giving of one's life, as the gospel explains. This redemptive self-sacrifice will heal our divided world.

After the Catonsville Nine action, Berrigan reflected on this truth in his book *No Bars to Manhood*:

We have assumed the name of peacemakers, but we have been, by and large, unwilling to pay any significant price. And because we want the peace with half a heart and half a life and will, the war, of course, continues, because the waging of war, by it nature, is total—but the waging of peace, by our own cowardice, is partial. So a whole will and a whole heart and a whole national life bent toward war prevail over the velleities of peace. . . . "Of course, let us have the peace," we cry, "but at the same time let us have normalcy, let us lose nothing, let our lives stand intact, let us know neither prison nor ill repute nor disruption of ties." . . . There is no peace because there are no peacemakers. There are no makers of peace because the making of peace is at least as costly as the making of war—at least as exigent, at least as disruptive, at least as liable to bring disgrace and prison and death in its wake.[13]

The giving of one's life for the promotion of life, as Jesus demonstrated, has become a central point in Berrigan's theology of nonviolent resistance. It is the challenge of the gospel that Berrigan reads for himself as well as for others. In his autobiography, he meditated on the call to lay down our lives as the heart of peacemaking:

The question for me, as peacemaking came to be a question, was one of soul, of center. The soul of peacemaking was simply the will to give one's life. As war sanctioned the taking of life, peacemaking must sanction the giving of life. Many believed (many still believe) that peace will come through a certain, nice adjustment of warmaking power, through diminished stockpiling, through a nuclear freeze. We still have not found our soul, or created a soul, or been granted a soul. We arrogate the metaphors and vocabulary of warmaking and call it peacemaking. For the warmakers want peace too, and always have. Which is to say, they seek a tolerable level of warmaking, one that will protect hegemonies and self-interest. And we too seek a certain level of peace—one that will protect our self-interest, modest as it may be; our ego; our good name in the world. We are still unable to attend to the considerable and central question—that of soul. Or more precisely, of the spiritual change required for peacemaking.[14]

While underground in 1970, he wrote, in *The Dark Night of Resistance*, "To cut free from the things people ordinarily give their hearts to, is not to lose the world, or the hearts of others, or the moral complicity with the fate of others which is all our longing and very nearly all our fate. No," he concludes, "it is to regain these things in a new way."[15]

Berrigan's reflections have been a theology-on-the-run, springing from a very active, public ministry of peacemaking. "By hook and crook, through clumsy and right thought, we were granted our own version of a base community, our own (perhaps in using the term dignify our efforts too much, we have yet to formulate things well) theology of resistance." From Central America, he wrote:

It has been a matter largely of reading as you run. We have had little help, in matters that seem to us of life-and-death import. We have yet to hear, after some twenty years of trial-and-error resistance, a word from a (male) North American theologian—a word indicating that our work offers a Christian insight into the times. (Women theologians, on the contrary, have been helpful in measure, especially Rosemary Ruether and Dorothee Solle). Does the situation amount to a mutual impoverishment? I think so.[16]

The church was first founded as a base community of nonviolent resistance, Berrigan suggests. Such a community was rooted in a new set of values, the values of Christ, and so there was no attachment to money, prestige, hatred, violence, and war. And yet, any such community, in a world of war and violence, would inevitably face great persecution and hostility from those dark forces. As Berrigan and his friends faced deeper persecution for their antiwar activity in the late 1960s, they began to reexplore the meaning of community and nonviolent resistance as a way of life.

The word *resistance* became very important around 1967 in the States. People were saying that it was necessary to take a step beyond protest. We could no longer look upon our style of life as merely being an occasion for this or that action. People had to begin thinking much more seriously and deeply about a long term struggle in which they would stand up more visibly and perhaps with more risk. Of course, people saw that transition in quite a different way. Some of the political activists said that a moral, individual action was no longer enough; there must be unity of effort which was more and more highly political. One person refusing induction or going on trial or leaving the university would have no impact. Now there must be a community behind him or her. . . . As a result of Catonsville and the draft board actions, people began to say that it was not enough to perform one action and disperse. People had to stay together preparing for trial, talking around the country, preparing legal defense, raising money, educating other people. . . . Communities of resistance were now required.[17]

Such communities have emerged around the gospel mandate of nonviolence in a time of violence. These communities have become a source of strength for a costly discipleship to Jesus which may involve arrest and imprisonment for opposition to nuclear weapons.

In New York City, where he lives and works with those dying of AIDS, Berrigan continues to meet with *Kairos*, a small local community of resisters. It meets regularly for prayer and discussions of political realities, "and then takes action in accord with what the group has learned together. Such actions in New York for a decade," he reports, "have included marching, fasting, leafleting, praying, and being arrested against official nuclear folly. And it's from a discipline like this that much of my recent writing has come. For instance, *The Nightmare of*

God issued from biblical and political discussions held, in and out of jail, in these past three years. So has a great deal of recent poetry."[18]

Berrigan's experience in prison has witnessed to the possibility of a deeper liberation for Americans caught in the web of consumerism and militarism. The journals and prison poems of his years in prison, especially *Lights on in the House of the Dead: A Prison Diary*, reveal that through the suffering he accepted and endured, he tasted the liberation of resurrection. He maintained his commitment to nonviolence, as well as a spirit of gentleness, patience, and joy. From his prison cell, he wrote, like St. Paul to the early communities, "One is to prefer, with Jesus, to suffer violence rather than inflict it."[19] Although in prison, Berrigan was free. His journal entry for October 20, 1970, listed the lessons he had learned from his own experiments in nonviolent resistance and his hopes for the future:

That what we do, that what we endure, will have meaning for others. That our lives are not wasted, in measure in which we give them. That the giving of our lives is a concrete, simple task; at center eye, the men we live with and suffer among and strive to serve. . . . That to be fools for Christ's sake is a responsible political position, given the rampant death society, its irresponsibility and horror of life. That we are called, as prisoners, to be disciplined, prayerful, constant, vigilant over sense and appetite, cheerful and of good heart. . . . That powerlessness is a way which offers solidarity and concurrent action with all those who struggle and endure in the world. That in prison we are in communion not only with suffering men and women of our world, but with the communion of saints in every time and place. That our jailers also lie under the scrutiny as well as the saving will of God, and stand in great need of our compassion and our courtesy—especially the large number of Catholics among them. That we are called to live the mystery of the cross and to sweat through the mystery of the resurrection. . . . That good humor and riding easy are the saving salt of our condition. We may win big, we may win small, we may lose everything. We can take whichever outcome. Important: stand where you must stand; be human there.[20]

The entry concludes: "I traced this on my cell wall (in Hebrew): Oasis of Peace." To see a prison cell in the United States as an "oasis of peace" is to experience the liberation of Christ's resurrection. In his prison cell, as his journal reveals, Berrigan painfully and gratefully received the risen Christ's gift of peace, and thus became an example for us all.

Berrigan is a biblical Christian who seeks the literal spirit of the Word and tries to apply it in the context of his own life and world. He notes the fundamentals of scripture: Jesus is compassionate, modest, loving, truthful, nonviolent, forgiving, and a steadfast resister of death. These fundamentals become the guideposts for his life of action, allowing him to speak with authenticity. "The Sermon on the Mount concerns us here and now; or concerns us never. In whatever modest and clumsy a way, we are called to honor the preference of Christ for suffering rather than inflicting suffering, for dying rather than killing; in that sense, all 'interim ethics' have been cast aside. The time to obey is now."[21] For Berrigan, the call to nonviolence and resistance is serious and urgent. If we are attentive to the Holy Spirit and open to its radical and challenging invitation, we will be led along the path of gospel peacemaking, as Berrigan has learned.

This desire to obey God's loving Spirit here and now regarding the most life-and-death realities of our time has brought Berrigan to such a deep faith and discipleship. His life message of truth and nonviolence has liberated many people from fear and apathy to experience the healing power of Christ's love in our world, and to allow that power to work in them to redeem the world. His advice to fellow Christians comes from years of following the inner voice of the Spirit. Become nonviolent resisters. Be messengers of truth. Be who you are: children of God, peacemakers. "Say things liberating, outrageous, provocative. Like: Christians are not allowed to kill or to be complicit in killing. Help us to a clarity that will be an immense political gift in a lousy time. Help us to a clear 'no' in place of a crepuscular 'maybe.'"[22]

By saying No to war and death, Berrigan hopes to say an even larger Yes to the God of life, the God of nonviolent love. "We are saved because this is the act of God in history: that we believe, and resist the forces of death. We resist because we believe; and we believe because we keep resisting," he observes.[23] By his example and his word, he has kept the faith and helped others to do likewise. Because of disciples like Daniel Berrigan, the day when nations will "beat swords into plowshares and study war no more" is surely close at hand.

Our God Is Nonviolent

Notes

1. John Deedy, *"Apologies, Good Friends:" An Interim Biography of Daniel Berrigan, S.J.* (Chicago: Fides/Claretian, 1981), 128–29.

2. Daniel Berrigan, "Swords into Plowshares," in Michael True, ed., *Daniel Berrigan: Poetry, Drama, Prose* (Maryknoll, N.Y.: Orbis Books, 1988), 182.

3. From remarks made at Kirkridge Retreat Center, in Bangor, Pennsylvania on January 14, 1984. Unpublished.

4. Ibid.

5. Ibid.

6. Daniel Berrigan, *To Dwell in Peace: An Autobiography* (San Francisco: Harper & Row, 1987), 174.

7. Ibid., 220.

8. Daniel Berrigan, "A Poet and a Priest," in Jim Wallis, ed., *Peacemakers* (San Francisco: Harper & Row, 1983), 149.

9. From remarks made at Fordham University on June 17, 1982. Unpublished.

10. Daniel Berrigan, "The Box Within a Box: A Tale of Chastened Expectations," in Dedria Bryfonski, ed., *Contemporary Authors: Autobiography Series*, vol. 1 (Detroit: Gale Research Co., 1984), 58.

11. From remarks made at Fordham University on June 17, 1982. Unpublished.

12. William O'Brien, "Daniel Berrigan: Portrait of the Peacemaker as a Healer," *The Other Side* (July/August 1987): 17.

13. Daniel Berrigan, *No Bars to Manhood* (New York: Bantam Books, 1970), 48–49.

14. Berrigan, *To Dwell in Peace*, 163–64.

15. Daniel Berrigan, *The Dark Night of Resistance* (New York: Doubleday Co., 1971), 171–72.

16. Daniel Berrigan, *Steadfastness of the Saints* (Maryknoll, N.Y.: Orbis Books, 1985), 23.

17. Daniel Berrigan, *The Raft Is Not the Shore* (Boston: Beacon Press, 1975), 121–22.

18. Berrigan, "The Box Within a Box," 54.

19. Daniel Berrigan, *Lights on in the House of the Dead: A Prison Diary* (New York: Doubleday & Co., 1974), 271.

20. Ibid., 40–41.

21. Daniel Berrigan, "The Peacemaker," in Patrick Hart, ed., *Thomas Merton/ Monk: A Monastic Tribute* (Kalamazoo, Mich.: Cistercian Pub., 1983), 226.

22. Daniel Berrigan, "Letter to the Editor: Elevated Mockery," *Commonweal* (July 17, 1987): 430.

23. Berrigan, "The Peacemaker," 227. For further information on the Plowshares movement, write to: Jonah House, 1933 Park Ave., Baltimore, MD 21217.

10

An Experience of Resistance and Nonviolence

THE STORY OF A BEGINNER

My three brothers and I grew up in Elizabeth City, a small town along the North Carolina coast. After years of schooling, travel, and odd jobs, I entered the Jesuits in the summer of 1982 with a desire to be a true follower of Jesus. I came to the order fresh from a private, prayerful pilgrimage to Israel. I had gone there to walk in the land of Jesus the peacemaker. I was shocked to discover the violent presence of the military everywhere—from the moment I stepped off the plane to face a soldier with a machine gun pointed at me, through the repressive actions I saw taken against the Palestinians while I was there, to the moment I left.

My prayerful walks in the Holy Land concluded with a week's stay along the Sea of Galilee. The high point of the experience came when I arrived at the Chapel of the Beatitudes, on a hill overlooking the Sea of Galilee. As I pondered the Sermon on the Mount and the call to gospel peacemaking, I wondered what it all meant for me. Just then, several sonic booms shook the land and two Israeli jets swooped down over the sea and directly over me, on their way to war in Lebanon. That day I decided to commit myself to the message of peace first delivered in Galilee. I went to the land of the Peacemaker only to witness a raging war and the urgent need for peace in our world.

In the Jesuit novitiate, time was given to prayer and the study of the scriptures, as well as to the study of the saints' lives. I took the opportunity to delve deep into the lives of modern-day saints—Gandhi, Martin Luther King, Jr., Dorothy Day, Thomas Merton, Oscar Romero, and others. It was a time of contemplation and study, balanced with action. We made the thirty-day silent retreat of St. Ignatius, the Spiritual Exercises. We were sent out to work with the poor—the homeless, disabled children, prisoners, the dying, Central American refugees. We were heading toward our goal: the profession of perpetual vows of poverty, chastity, obedience in community, and for some of us, nonviolence, and a new life of dedicated service to humanity.

Part of the Jesuit training involved a six-month assignment with a Jesuit community. I was sent to Washington, D.C., where I worked with Salvadoran refugee children. While there, another novice and I decided to go to the Pentagon and test for ourselves the truth of the gospel. We wanted to do our own Gandhian experiments in truth.

It was Lent. We made up our minds to go to the Pentagon early in the morning once a week to witness for peace. Each week we would do something different, but our action would be public. The results would be unknown to us, and out of our hands. The point, we decided, was to witness, in the old-fashioned sense; to speak to those we met with love and respect about the Lenten message of repentance and nonviolence.

Neither of us had ever done anything like this before and it proved to be eye-opening. We were a bit nervous and apprehensive. On the evening prior to our first witness, we prayed and planned. We wrote a leaflet in the form of a memo, titled, "To the Women and Men who work at the Pentagon; Re: the Coming of the Kingdom of God." It concluded with a bold request: "We ask in the name of Jesus Christ, the one whom many of you confess as Lord and Savior, to abandon your present participation in the institutionalized violence of the military establishment and 'Come and follow Jesus.' "

Sometimes, we stood silently on the Pentagon steps and prayed. Usually, we tried to speak with Pentagon employees about the nonviolent alternative. One time, we approached employees as they entered the building and begged them to go home, to quit their jobs, "for God's sake." After the initial shock and surprise, some people struck back with anger. "You ought to be ashamed of yourselves," they said. The police were called, and we were ordered to leave the grounds or face arrest for disturbing the peace.

After Easter, I decided to continue the witness by sitting down in one of the doorways as an expression of loving disobedience to the work of the Pentagon. It would be a simple, peaceful, symbolic, public expression of dissent. While I knew that in the eyes of the world—even in my own eyes—it seemed ridiculous, I felt a call to act.

My action became for me a moment of grace, a spiritual moment of prayer, realized in personal risk. I read from the scriptures and prayed for the people of the Pentagon and for the victims of the work of the Pentagon. I prayed that God might forgive us all and have mercy on us. I prayed for all humanity and for the church, for its conversion to nonviolence. I offered up the whole experience of resistance to God.

Soon I found myself surrounded by six police officers carrying guns and clubs. I was arrested, handcuffed, loaded into a police van, and carted off to be fingerprinted and booked.

Two months later, I stood before a magistrate in the county courthouse in Alexandria, Virginia. "I went to the Pentagon," I told the magistrate, "in response to the direction our country is going with its billion-dollar defense system, nuclear weapons production, and support of violence in countries around the world—all of which oppress Americans and people around the world. I have never been arrested before and have no desire to go to jail, but rather, I acted in conscience. . . . To the charge of blocking the entrance, I plead guilty and I am guilty, but technically there were many other doors and many people passed by me freely, on either side of me.

"I had been asking myself for months," I continued, "when does the time come for a person to stop compromising, to stop blaming others for the violence in the world; when is it time for a person to put his or her body on the line—in love for the poor and suffering of the world and say No to the preparation for war? I have concluded that now is the time for everyone, including myself, to act in faith for others. I found myself no longer able to stand by idly while my government continued to support and plan the use of violence. My sitting down was a loud No to violence and a Yes to peace, truth, nonviolence, and forgiveness.

"I am greatly distressed and disturbed that $1.5 million are spent on nuclear weapons and violence every minute [the 1984 figure] around the world while at the same time over forty-five thousand people die of dramatic starvation every day. The Pentagon symbolizes and represents the study and propagation of violence in the world.

"I am twenty-four years old and plan to profess perpetual vows of poverty, chastity, and obedience in August in the Society of Jesus. This Society of Jesus of which I am a member gathered at its recent congregation in October, 1983—with every province sending members to represent the twenty-six thousand members around the world—and committed itself forever 'to that work which is the promotion of a more just world order, greater solidarity of rich countries with poor, and a lasting peace based on human rights and freedom.' Many of my brother Jesuits witness through nonviolence for 'international justice and an end to an arms race that deprives the poor and threatens to destroy civilization.'

"May I say that I am a Christian," I added, "a follower of Jesus Christ, who was killed by the authorities for speaking out against violence and proclaiming the reign of God through love and truth. . . . The week I was arrested was Easter week. Christians around the world had just celebrated Holy Week—remembering the crucifixion of Jesus Christ and his resurrection. As a Christian, I hoped that I would be able to share in the arrest, abuse, and sufferings of Jesus Christ, my Lord and my God. As his follower, and with my brother Jesuits, I seek to imitate him, to practice active nonviolent love for others, and to serve all people in truth and in love. As a Christian, I desire to lay down my life for others—even in simple ways like sitting down in Pentagon doorways—and I will accept the consequences for what I see as the truth.

"My action symbolically shows my dissent with the direction our country is taking," I concluded, "and is in keeping with the ideals of the Society of Jesus and my faith in God. I hope my action will encourage others to work for peace through nonviolence, to serve the poor in an effort to love one another, and to stand up or sit down in opposition to violence and the preparation of war and in affirmation of peace and love and faith in God. In the end, I am simply trying to be faithful to my God who is nonviolent and forgiving, and to witness to the truth, to nonviolence, and to the resurrection of Jesus of Nazareth."

The magistrate listened to my remarks and responded that my purpose was indeed noble. "However," he said, "the law is the law and you have broken it. Therefore, I sentence you to thirty days in jail. Since this is your first offense, I suspend the sentence and put you on a one-year probation." I was free to go.

The experiments in truth continued. I moved to the Bronx, in New York City, to study philosophy as part of the Jesuit course, and also worked at a soup kitchen and a shelter for the homeless. I joined *Kairos*, a base community of friends and resisters who had been working for years to raise questions about the arms race.

In 1985, I traveled to Central America where I lived in one of El Salvador's refugee camps, part soup kitchen, part shelter, part hospital. But it was more than that: it was a farm, a school, and, most important, a church community. We prayed together and laughed together and shared stories with one another. But in the distance, the war blazed on furiously: bombs were dropped every day by U.S. aircraft on nearby villages and machine-gun fire could be heard regularly. I was questioned on several occasions by death squad soldiers. In Guatemala and Nicaragua, I saw more effects of the U.S.-supported wars in that region. I spent a few weeks in Nicaragua near the Honduran border, visiting families living in terrible poverty who were victims of the U.S.-backed contra war. Everywhere I went, the message of the people was clear: Tell your people this: Send bread not bombs. Stop the war against us.

Back in the United States, I returned to the Pentagon, this time to meet the Secretary of the Army, John Marsh, who was a friend of my father. In his office, which is filled with murals of bloody battle scenes from the American Revolution, I spoke about what I had seen and heard. I asked him to stop the violence of United States intervention throughout Central America. He replied that he would not as long as the threat of communism hung over the region. I left saddened and angry that once again, war was being justified in the name of anticommunism, a catch-all phrase very popular with all Western warriors from Adolf Hitler to Ferdinand Marcos to Ronald Reagan. As always, the so-called communists, the victims of this word game, were simple peasant farmers trying to survive the injustice of poverty.

In the Bronx, some friends alerted me to an invitation to go to the United States Military Academy at West Point to talk with the cadets and distribute leaflets about the consequences of American imperialism and violence toward the poor of Central America. Many of us participated in that peaceful witness; three of us decided to walk into the private courtyard of the main dormitory to continue distributing leaflets. We gave out our message and talked with many cadets.

Then a commander approached us: "Stand right here!" he said. "Why?" we asked. He repeated his order, but we continued our leafleting. Within seconds we were handcuffed and searched. The three of us began reciting the Lord's Prayer. When we arrived at police headquarters, we were questioned, photographed, fingerprinted, videotaped, and told repeatedly to stop singing. "We apologize for any inconvenience we may have cost you," my friends and I said to those who guarded us. "We want you to know that we bear no ill will toward you. We're doing this on behalf of the poor of Central America." "That's all right," the guards inevitably responded, with disarming smiles.

We were detained for several hours, and sat handcuffed in a waiting room overlooking the Hudson River. The view was breathtaking. In those quiet hours, I was able to reflect on the lessons of Jesus and the witness of Gandhi: Be willing to suffer for justice' sake; love your enemies; be nonviolent; accept poverty voluntarily. In a spirit of emptiness and compassion, a deep peace came upon each of us.

Back in New York City, as my studies and work with the homeless progressed, our *Kairos* group pressed on with the campaign at the Riverside Research Institute, a Star Wars think tank in downtown Manhattan. The institute has been preparing for first-strike nuclear war for years, and recently it has become a leading center for the Pentagon's so-called Strategic Defense Initiative. We leafleted outside the think tank for years, and on holy days we publicly protested the work that goes on there by sitting down in the lobby and blocking the entrance to one of the doorways. Every Good Friday, thousands of Christians walked across Manhattan, beginning at the United Nations, leafleting, praying, and singing all the way. These modern stations of the cross included stops at the army recruiting center at Times Square and at pornography shops. The fifteenth station, in honor of Christ's resurrection, is commemorated with a sit-in at Riverside Research Institute. Each year scores of people are arrested.

On the forty-second anniversary of the bombing of Hiroshima, twenty-five of us were arrested for blocking the entrance to the Riverside Research Institute. Another twenty-five kept vigil, leafleted, and sang. We tried to show the institute employees our respect for them and sought ways to speak with them. Protesters arrested that day were taken to the local precinct, issued summonses, and released. Then, three of us went back and began again.

New York police officers are used to arresting people at the Riverside Research Institute. While they are polite and courteous because they recognize the nonviolent character of the demonstrations and the good spirit of the group, they are upset when we go back and act again on the same day.

On that Hiroshima day, we were brought back into the police station and the lieutenant in charge seemed perplexed at our recidivism. He said we would regret our double action because he was going to put us through "the system." For the next twenty-four hours we were routed through New York City's jails, precincts, and holding cells. We saw hundreds of police officers and hundreds of prisoners: nearly all the officers were white, and, except for us, all the prisoners black. We discovered the institutionalization of racism and sexism in the bowels of the city.

As we were bused around town and held, handcuffed, in crowded cells, our fellow prisoners asked what we had done. We spoke of our strong desire to close down Riverside Research Institute and all other such places and to follow in the steps of Jesus and Martin Luther King, Jr. They were very supportive of us, but many, on the brink of despair, said that they had given up pursuing justice. As one fellow said, "Look around here: we all make lousy criminals. We're survivors, just trying to get by." Most of the men had been arrested for robbery or drug dealing and would pay a price for their deeds. But there are larger crimes of war and money being committed on Wall Street and in the government each day, and the prisoners knew it.

Most of the police officers in the "system," on the other hand, had only contempt for my friends and me, and for all prisoners in the system. They took great pleasure in mocking us, along with the others. Here, a person was no longer considered a human being. When I asked the young officer who was fingerprinting me how he managed to maintain his self-respect and integrity while ignoring our humanity and individual worth, he looked at the crowded cell and responded, "Those dogs are not human beings." By dehumanizing us, they could justify treating us inhumanely.

In the late evening, we were chained together, crammed into a small van, and driven from precinct to precinct, searching for a jail with room for all of us. The heat inside the van was overwhelming. Finally, we were brought to a jail in Harlem. We were divided into pairs to share four-by-eight-foot cells built originally for one person. There was a long bench and a toilet in each cell; everything stank of urine. The cell doors were slammed shut, my cell-mate collapsed into sleep, and I began a long solitary vigil.

Being in the Harlem jail was living a paradox. It was horrible—filthy, dehumanizing. And yet, it was a glorious experience. My mind filled with images of Henry David Thoreau's one night in jail, Dr. King's repeated jailings, Gandhi's long prison terms, the Vietnam war resisters, Dorothy Day, and Franz Jagerstatter, the Austrian peasant jailed and beheaded for refusing to fight in Hitler's army. I thought of the hundreds of people around the country also jailed that night for protesting the nuclear arms race. I thought of Jesus' long night in the Jerusalem jail, awaiting trial, torture, and public execution.

I thought of all the people killed forty-two years before in those fire-blasts at Hiroshima and Nagasaki.

Those late-night thoughts in the Harlem jail led me to a new sense of religious freedom. It was right for me to be there on such a day, on such a night, in such an age. Earlier, I had used the chains that attached us prisoners together as rosary beads. Now in the nonviolence and prayerfulness of our action, in the midst of such a place, God seemed very present to me in the spirit of peace.

That day and night of resistance was an experience of spiritual freedom. It proved to me that all the way to liberation is liberating; that all the way to peace is peaceful; and that all the way to nonviolent love is an experience of nonviolent love.

The willingness to suffer, to be arrested, to go to jail, to be killed— all for the sake of justice and peace—is essential if we are to create a world of justice and peace. This willingness to suffer for justice' sake— to take up the cross—is necessary if one is to experience the peace the risen Christ came to give. It is at the heart of love—the willingness to lay down one's life for one's friends.

My own journey from Elizabeth City, North Carolina, to Washington, D.C., to Galilee, to the Jesuit Novitiate in Pennsylvania, to the Pentagon, to the Bronx, to El Salvador, Nicaragua, and Guatemala, to West Point, and eventually to a night in the Harlem jail has been rich with moments of resurrection. Along the way I have discovered a God who asks us to resist evil, and to resist nonviolently, showing love for all. This great God, who proves to be divine through such tremendous nonviolent love, beckons all of us to be like God, to be nonviolent and loving. It is an invitation we can no longer resist.

The Challenge Is Ours

A CONCLUSION

When we look around the world with eyes wide open, we see pain and poverty, despair and violence, evil beyond belief. The scene is a nightmare. What can we do? What can we say? We are tempted to weep and weep; we feel the urge to pray constantly for God's mercy. And so, we weep and pray.

Through all this, there is reason to hope and reason to believe in God's mercy. Jesus' life and death reveal the power of nonviolent love which resists and then overcomes evil. Jesus died on the cross for his acts of resistance to the ruling authority; but his resurrection is sign from heaven of God's great power to transform all into new life. God's way of transformation is through loving, nonviolent resistance. It is a challenging way that requires us to commit our very lives, as God requires the very heart and soul of each one of us. God is nonviolent and loving and resists evil. God is not passive, but very active in the world, and so God is very demanding. God wants to transform all war and injustice into peace and justice, but God wants to work through us to do it.

The good news is that every one of us can live the life of Jesus, share in his resurrection, and help God transform the world by committing ourselves to the same faith and hope and Spirit of nonviolent love. Every one of us can enter the kingdom of God, the kingdom of nonviolent love. All we have to do is practice active, nonviolent love; we have to stand up to the forces of evil and risk our very lives to insist on justice and peace. We are invited to a selflessness that accepts suffering, prison, and death for the struggle of a new world—God's kingdom. All we have to do is follow Jesus' way of life.

The world of violence will not be transformed easily. It will defend its cruelty in every way it can. When Jesus confronted the symbol of worldly power in the Jerusalem temple, he was quickly arrested, jailed, condemned, tortured, and executed. The gospel invites us to take up where he left off. Jesus' way of the cross, a way of public confrontation and loving disobedience to the evil practices of society, will lead to transformation and resurrection, but it will cost us everything, as it did with him.

Today, the nuclear arms race—the crucifixion of humanity—is legal; capital punishment is legal; abortion is legal. The murder of Nicaraguan and Salvadoran children is legal. The crucifixion of Jesus was also legal. But Jesus' resurrection was illegal—he went past the Roman soldiers guarding his tomb and went out to encourage his followers to continue the work of love and resistance. Jesus acted illegally to transform evil into goodness and continued that work by rising from the dead, an illegal act. To be more faithful today, we need to get on the side of the troublemaking, illegal Jesus. We need to become troublemakers. The risen Christ invites us to the troublesome, uncomfortable work that publicly challenges the ruling authorities that get away with murder.

A measure of discipleship, it has been said, is the amount of trouble that we are in, the persecution that we face from the ruling authorities of society. As true disciples of the unarmed, illegal Christ, we will be in trouble with the powers and principalities of the world.

Why will we be in trouble? We will be in trouble for speaking the truth. We will be in trouble for inciting people to claim only God as their security—not nuclear weapons, not ideologies, not a comfortable life style. We will be in trouble for opposing payment of taxes to the warmaking state, as well as for opposing its wars, its love of death, its injustices, its apartheids—foreign and domestic. We will be in trouble for being in trouble. We will be in trouble because we claim to be children of God; we claim that everyone is a child of God. We claim to be followers of Jesus. We believe in Jesus Christ; thus, we claim God's reign of justice, truth, and nonviolence over us. We will be in trouble for loving all people on earth and for our efforts to bring them into God's kingdom of justice and nonviolent love.

As we can expect trouble for our nonviolent resistance, our revolutionary gentle love, we can also expect to rise and to enter more fully into the truth, the nonviolent reign of God with Jesus. With this great hope—the hope that we can read between the lines of Jesus' last words on the cross—we can rightly walk forward, here in the United States, as followers of Jesus, offering the gift of our lives, walking for justice and peace, walking with and for the poor, the oppressed, and the victims of our government's policies; walking on behalf of the unborn and those on death row; walking with the homeless, the hungry, the gays and lesbians, the oppressed women and children of the world, the refugees, the Nicaraguan people, the Russians, all the poor of the world; standing up against the principalities and powers of death, against all the forces of darkness in this world that seek to do violence and to kill.

God has shown us through the death and resurrection of Jesus that when we live lives of nonviolent love and resistance to evil, our survival is guaranteed. God will raise us body and soul into eternal life; all we are asked to do is practice nonviolent love. In great hope, then, we can continue to walk forward, to resist death, and to choose life, come what may. With this hope, we can go public with our love for all peoples of the world—especially the poor—and walk forward into God's reign of love and justice.

This walk of nonviolent resistance with our nonviolent God is a road to freedom. The One who has gone ahead of us beckons us to join him on the journey. In hope and love, let us take up the lifelong, life-giving Christian task of nonviolent resistance.

SUGGESTED READING

Aldridge, Robert C. *First Strike! The Pentagon's Strategy for Nuclear War*. Boston: South End Press, 1983.
————. *Nuclear Empire*. Vancouver: New Star Books, 1989.
Berrigan, Daniel. *Uncommon Prayer*. New York: Winston/Seabury, 1978.
————. *The Nightmare of God*. Portland, Oreg.: Sunburst Press, 1983.
————. *To Dwell in Peace*. San Francisco: Harper & Row, 1987.
Berrigan, Philip. *Widen the Prison Gates*. New York: Simon & Schuster, 1973.
Berrigan, Philip, and McAlister, Elizabeth. *The Time's Discipline: The Beatitudes and Nuclear Resistance*. Baltimore: Fortkamp Pub., 1989.
Bondurant, Joan V. *Conquest of Violence*. Berkeley: University of California Press, 1958.
Bonhoeffer, Dietrich. *The Cost of Discipleship*. New York: Macmillan Co., 1953.
Brockman, James R. *The Word Remains: A Life of Oscar Romero*. Maryknoll, N.Y.: Orbis Books, 1982.
Camara, Helder. *The Spiral of Violence*. New York: Sheed & Ward, 1971.
Carrigan, Ana. *Salvador Witness: The Life and Calling of Jean Donovan*. New York: Simon & Schuster, 1983.
Chapman, G. Clarke. *Facing the Nuclear Heresy*. Elgin, Ill.: Brethren Press, 1986.
Day, Dorothy. *The Long Loneliness*. San Francisco: Harper & Row, 1981.
————. *Loaves and Fishes*. San Francisco: Harper & Row, 1963.
Dear, John. *Disarming the Heart: Toward a Vow of Nonviolence*. Mahwah, N.J.: Paulist Press, 1987.

Suggested Reading

————. *Jean Donovan: The Call to Discipleship.* Erie, Pa.: Pax Christi U.S.A., 1986.

Dear, John, with Hines, Joe, eds. *Christ Is With the Poor: Stories and Sayings of Horace McKenna, S.J.* Washington, D.C., 1989. Available from: McKenna Center, 19 Eye Street, N.W., Washington, D.C. 20001.

Dietrich, Jeff. *Reluctant Resister.* Greensboro, N.C.: Unicorn Press, 1983.

Douglass, James W. *The Nonviolent Cross.* New York: Macmillan Co., 1969.

————. *Resistance and Contemplation.* New York: Doubleday & Co., 1972.

————. *Lightning East to West.* New York: Crossroad, 1983.

Easwaran, Eknath. *Gandhi the Man.* Berkeley: Nilgiri Press, 1978.

Ellsberg, Robert, ed. *By Little and By Little: The Selected Writings of Dorothy Day.* New York: Alfred A. Knopf, 1983.

Finney, Torin. *Unsung Hero of the Great War: The Life and Witness of Ben Salmon.* Mahwah, N.J.: Paulist Press, 1989.

Fischer, Louis. *The Life of Mahatma Gandhi.* New York: Harper & Row, 1954.

Forest, Jim. *Love Is the Measure: A Biography of Dorothy Day.* Mahwah, N.J.: Paulist Press, 1986.

Gutierrez, Gustavo. *A Theology of Liberation.* Maryknoll, N.Y.: Orbis Books, 1973.

————. *We Drink from Our Own Wells.* Maryknoll, N.Y.: Orbis Books, 1983.

Hanh, Thich Nhat. *Being Peace.* Berkeley: Parallax Press, 1987.

Hauerwas, Stanley. *The Peaceable Kingdom.* Notre Dame, Ind.: Univ. of Notre Dame Press, 1983.

Hersey, John. *Hiroshima.* New York: Alfred A. Knopf, 1946.

Hollyday, Joyce. *Turning Toward Home.* San Francisco: Harper & Row, 1989.

Jesudasan, Ignatius. *A Gandhian Theology of Liberation.* Maryknoll, N.Y.: Orbis Books, 1984.

Kaku, Michio, and Axelrod, Daniel. *To Win a Nuclear War: The Pentagon's Secret War Plans.* Boston: South End Press, 1987.

Kavanaugh, John. *Following Christ in a Consumer Society.* Maryknoll, N.Y.: Orbis Books, 1983.

Laffin, Arthur J., and Montgomery, Anne. *Swords into Plowshares.* San Francisco: Harper & Row, 1987.

McGinnis, James and Kathleen. *Parenting for Peace and Justice.* Maryknoll, N.Y.: Orbis Books, 1981.

McSorley, Richard. *New Testament Basis for Peacemaking.* Scottdale, Pa.: Herald Press, 1985.

Merton, Thomas. *Gandhi on Nonviolence.* New York: New Directions, 1965.

————. *The Hidden Ground of Love: Letters.* Ed. William Shannon. New York: Farrar, Straus & Giroux, 1985.

————. *The Nonviolent Alternative.* New York: Farrar, Straus & Giroux, 1980.

————. *The Road to Joy: Letters.* Ed. Robert Daggy. New York: Farrar, Straus & Giroux, 1989.

Suggested Reading

Musto, Ronald G. *The Catholic Peace Tradition*. Maryknoll, N.Y.: Orbis Books, 1986.

Myers, Ched. *Binding the Strong Man: A Political Reading of Mark's Story of Jesus*. Maryknoll, N.Y.: Orbis Books, 1988.

Romero, Oscar. *The Violence of Love: The Pastoral Wisdom of Oscar Romero*. Comp. James Brockman. San Francisco: Harper & Row, 1988.

Schell, Jonathan. *The Fate of the Earth*. New York: Alfred A. Knopf, 1981.

Schussler Fiorenza, Elisabeth. *In Memory of Her: A Feminist Theological Reconstruction of Christian Origins*. New York: Crossroad, 1985.

Shannon, William. *Seeking the Face of God*. New York: Crossroad, 1988.

Solle, Dorothee. *Of War and Love*. Maryknoll, N.Y.: Orbis Books, 1981.

Stringfellow, William. *An Ethic for Christians and Other Aliens in a Strange Land*. Waco, Tex.: Word, 1973.

————. *Politics of Spirituality*. Philadelphia: Westminster Press, 1984.

Swartley, Willard. *Slavery, Sabbath, War and Women*. Scottdale, Pa.: Herald Press, 1983.

Taylor, Richard, and Sider, Ronald. *Nuclear Holocaust and Christian Hope*. Downers Grove, Ill.: Intervarsity, 1982.

Tolstoy, Leo. *On Civil Disobedience and Nonviolence*. New York: Bergman Pub., 1967.

Trocme, Andre. *Jesus and the Nonviolent Revolution*. Scottdale, Pa.: Herald Press, 1973.

True, Michael, ed. *Daniel Berrigan: Poetry, Drama, Prose*. Maryknoll, N.Y.: Orbis Books, 1988.

Wallis, Jim. *Agenda for Biblical People*. San Francisco: Harper & Row, 1984.

————. *Waging Peace*. New York: Harper & Row, 1982.

————. *Peacemakers*. San Francisco: Harper & Row, 1983.

————. *The Rise of Christian Conscience*. San Francisco: Harper & Row, 1987.

Washington, James M. *A Testament of Hope: The Essential Writings of Martin Luther King, Jr*. San Francisco: Harper & Row, 1986.

Welch, Sharon. *Communities of Resistance and Solidarity: A Feminist Theology of Liberation*. Maryknoll, N.Y.: Orbis Books, 1985.

Wink, Walter. *Violence and Nonviolence in South Africa: Jesus' Third Way*. Philadelphia: New Society Pub., 1987.

————. *Naming the Powers*. Philadelphia: Fortress Press, 1984.

————. *Unmasking the Powers*. Philadelphia: Fortress Press, 1987.

Yoder, John Howard. *The Politics of Jesus*. Grand Rapids, Mich.: Wm. B. Eerdmans, 1972.

Zahn, Gordan. *In Solitary Witness: The Life and Death of Franz Jagerstatter*. Philadelphia: Templegate, 1986.